CONSPIRACY:
A BIBLICAL VIEW

Other Books by Gary North

Marx's Religion of Revolution (1968, 1989)
An Introduction to Christian Economics (1973)
Puritan Economic Experiments (1974, 1988)
Unconditional Surrender (1981, 1988, 1994)
Successful Investing in an Age of Envy (1981)
The Dominion Covenant: Genesis (1982, 1987)
Government by Emergency (1983)
Backward, Christian Soldiers? (1984)
75 Bible Questions Your Instructors Pray You Won't Ask (1984)
Coined Freedom (1984)
Moses and Pharaoh (1985)
The Sinai Strategy (1986)
Conspiracy: A Biblical View (1986)
Honest Money (1986)
Fighting Chance (1986), with Arthur Robinson
Unholy Spirits: Occultism & New Age Humanism (1986)
Dominion and Common Grace (1987)
Inherit the Earth (1987)
Liberating Planet Earth (1987)
Healer of the Nations (1987)
The Pirate Economy (1987)
Is the World Running Down? (1988)
When Justice Is Aborted (1989)
Political Polytheism (1989)
The Hoax of Higher Criticism (1990)
Tools of Dominion: The Case Laws of Exodus (1990)
Victim's Rights (1990)
Westminster's Confession (1991)
Christian Reconstruction (1991), with Gary DeMar
The Coase Theorem (1992)
Politically Incorrect (1993)
Salvation Through Inflation (1993)
Rapture Fever (1993)
Tithing and the Church (1994)
Leviticus: An Economic Commentary (1994)
Baptized Patriarchalism (1995)
Crossed Fingers: How the Liberals Captured the Presbyterian Church (1996)

CONSPIRACY
A Biblical View

Gary North

Dominion Press
Tyler, Texas

Library of Congress Cataloging-in-Publication Data

North, Gary
  Conspiracy : a biblical view / Gary North. – 2nd ed.

  Originally written as the prologue and epilogue to: Call It
Conspiracy / Larry Abraham. c1985. Then it was published as
a separate work, slightly revised in 1986. This edition is minus
one chapter from the original.

  Includes bibliographical references and index.

  ISBN 0-930462-11-4

  1. Dominion theology. 2. History (Theology). 3. Conspiracies.
  4. International organization. 5. Council on Foreign Relations.
  6. Trilateral Commission. 7. World politics–20th century.
  8. United States–Politics and government–20th century.
  9. Decentralization in government.   I. Title

BT82.25.N673 1996   96-24984
909.82–dc20   CIP

Published by:
Dominion Press
P. O. Box 7999
Tyler, TX 75711

This book is dedicated to

Antony Sutton
Otto Scott - *"the silent majority"*

who did their homework,
published their findings,
and paid the price.

TABLE OF CONTENTS

PREFACE

It lies within the power of the Atlantic communities to impose peace upon the world and secure unimpeded movement and free speech from end to end of the earth. This is a fact on which the Open Conspiracy must insist. The English-speaking states, France, Germany, Holland, Switzerland, the Scandinavian countries and Russia, given not only a not very extravagant frankness of understanding between them, and a common disposition towards the idea of the Open Conspiracy, could cease to arm against each other and still exert enough strength to impose disarmament and a respect for human freedom in every corner of the planet. It is fantastic pedantry to wait for all the world to accede before all the world is pacified and policed.

H. G. Wells (1928)[1]

There is in the hearts of men the impulse to extend their control over others. The quest for power is an ancient one. When the quest for power is fused with the humanitarian quest to do good for others, whether they want it done for them or not, it becomes difficult to resist. And when both impulses are joined with the ability to become fabulously wealthy in the process, and to pass this wealth down to one's heirs, both biological and spiritual, the lure becomes almost irresistible. <u>To do well while doing good</u>: what a marvelous opportunity!

---

1. H. G. Wells, *The Open Conspiracy: Blue Prints for a World Revolution* (Garden City, New York: Doubleday, Doran, 1928), pp. 189–90.

or in some cases the Church

But it takes power to achieve this comprehensive goal: the power of the <u>State</u>. Herbert George Wells—socialist, novelist, and sexual libertine—understood this as well as anyone ever has. The visionary's price of universal wealth for all is the surrender of national sovereignty to a new world political order.

Tower of Babel

> The realisation of this conceivable better order involves certain necessary achievements. It is impossible for any clear-headed person to suppose that the ever more destructive stupidities of war can be eliminated from human affairs until some common political control dominates the earth, and unless certain pressures due to the growth of population, due to the enlarging scope of human operations or due to conflicting standards and traditions of life, are disposed of. To avoid the positive evils of war and to attain the new levels of prosperity and power that now come into view, an effective world control, not merely of armed force but of the production and main movements of staple commodities and the drift and expansion of population, is required. It is absurd to dream of peace and world-wide progress without that much control. These things assured, the abilities and energies of a greatly increased proportion of human beings could be diverted to the happy activities of scientific research and creative work with an ever-increasing release and enlargement of human possibility. Such a forward stride in human life, the first stride in a mighty continuing advance, an advance to which no limit appears, is now materially possible. The opportunity is offered to mankind. But there is no certainty, no material necessity, that it should ever be taken. It will not be taken by mankind inadvertently. It can only be taken through such an organisation of will and energy to take it as this world has never seen before.[2]

In other words, the creation of this new world order must be planned. It must be planned by a conspiracy. He called it the open conspiracy in 1928. A dozen years later, he was still call-

---

2. *Ibid.*, pp. 24–25.

ing for world socialism in the post-war world. In his book, *The New World Order*, he proclaimed: "Can one doubt that the 'scientific world' will break out in this way when the revolution is achieved, and that the development of man's power over nature and over his own nature and over this still unexplored planet, will undergo a continual acceleration as the years pass? No man can guess beforehand what doors will open then nor upon what wonderlands."[3] A grand vision, indeed!

Six years later, his faith was in tatters. In *Mind at the End of Its Tether*, he lamented: "The end of everything we call life is close at hand and cannot be evaded."[4] Ours is a closed universe, yet we need something beyond it. " 'Power' is unsatisfactory."[5] He had seen where the evolutionary process was leading and had to lead: to the death of man. "Man must go steeply up or down and the odds seem to be all in favour of his going down and out. If he goes up, then so great is the adaptation demanded of him that he must cease to be a man. Ordinary man is at the end of his tether. Only a small, highly adaptable minority of the species can possibly survive."[6]

Did this bring him to adopt a new worldview? Did it bring him back to his youthful faith in God? Hardly. In a simultaneously published book, he rejoiced in his life of blasphemy. "From first to last I have invented a considerable amount of excellent blasphemy."[7] Christianity was still his greatest enemy: ". . . I recognise and deal with these Christian teachers for the foolish weaklings they are. I refuse to accept this consecrated riff-raff as my moral and mental equals. Clearly they are either knaves or fools or a blend in various proportions of the two, and to treat them as though they were intelligent honest men

---

3. Wells, *The New World Order* (London: Secker & Warburg, 1940), p. 189.

4. Wells, *Mind at the End of Its Tether* (New York: Didier, 1946), p. 1.

5. *Ibid.*, p. 12.

6. *Ibid.*, p. 30.

7. Wells, *The Happy Turning: A Dream of Life* (New York: Didier, 1946), p. 6.

even the Socialist mind may recognize the inherent sinfulness of man.

in this world crisis, becomes a politeness treasonable to man-kind."[8] He died shortly thereafter.

Wells understood the nature of the culture war he was in. He was a proponent of a new world order, one in which an international government would impose its will on other governments and all men, all for their own good. He was quite forthright: the protests of those governed against their will would be in vain. "It is fantastic pedantry to wait for all the world to accede before all the world is pacified and policed." He also understood that there was a threat to this new world order: Christianity. Most of his final book was a fantasy about meeting Jesus in a world of dreams. This Jesus was disgusted with all of His followers. "Gods! how he hated priests, and how he hates them now! And Paul!"[9]

Wells knew that those who defend the kingdom of God in history would eventually recognize the threat posed by a humanistic one-world order. It might take time, but resistance would come. Christianity therefore had to be challenged, undermined, and destroyed.

What Wells understood, his fellow conspirators also understand. Christians, as always, have been the last to hear. This has been true from the beginning. The religious authorities of Israel worried that the disciples would try to steal Jesus' body and announce His resurrection after three days (Matthew 27:62–66). They fully understood His prophesies; meanwhile, the disciples had scattered. The resurrection came as a surprise to them. But eventually, they learned. Then they became an even greater threat than the authorities had imagined.

Today, at long last, a growing minority of Christians has begun to understand the theological and organizational nature of the cultural and civilizational war they are in, and have long been in, unbeknownst to most of their predecessors. For exam-

---

8. *Ibid.*, pp. 42–43.
9. *Ibid.*, p. 14.

ple, Pat Robertson's book, *The New World Order* (1991), spelled out at least some of the historical details in Part 2. He quotes Richard Gardner, Ph.D., a Rhodes Scholar and high-level functionary in the Kennedy-Johnson State Department: "In short, the 'house of world order' will have to be built from the bottom up rather than from the top down. . . . An end run around national sovereignty, eroding it piece by piece, will accomplish much more than the old fashioned assault."[10] Gardner announced this in *Foreign Affairs* (April 1974), the influential publication of the Council on Foreign Relations (C.F.R.).

Gardner's declaration reveals that the vision articulated by H. G. Wells is still alive and well. So is the officially admitted strategy: an open conspiracy. If you are going to run a conspiracy, put some of it into the open so that the targeted victims think they are seeing all of it. But Robertson was rocking the boat by going to the publications of this conspiracy and quoting verbatim some of its more outrageous declarations. For having written *The New World Order*, he was denounced and ridiculed in the press, which had previously ignored his books.

Robertson, the son of a U.S. Senator who was chairman of the Senate Banking Committee, came to this awareness rather late in his career, but the fact that he has come is significant. He was not the first to do so, but he is surely the only one with his own television network and law school to do so.

Whose New World Order?

I wrote the bulk of this book as the Prologue and Epilogue to Larry Abraham's *Call It Conspiracy*, which was published in 1985. I then revised it slightly and published it as a separate book in 1986. It was co-distributed by Crossway Books and my company, Dominion Press, later in 1986. I have decided to release it again, minus one chapter, " 'Convergence': Justifying

---

10. Cited in Robertson, *The New World Order* (Dallas: Word, 1991), p. 6.

Surrender." With the collapse of the Soviet Union in 1991, there was no further need for a chapter on the foreign policy establishment's long-term pressures to bring together the Soviet Union and the United States under a common one-world government.

The issue here is the new world order. Jesus Christ inaugurated a New World Order. His followers call it the New Covenant. No other world order will ever replace it. But there are rival orders and would-be orders. They have their spokesmen.

On September 11, 1990, President George Bush delivered a speech to Congress. He made these observations:

> A new partnership of nations has begun. We stand today at a unique and extraordinary moment. The crisis in the Persian Gulf, as grave as it is, also offers a rare opportunity to move toward an historic period of cooperation. Out of these troubled times, our fifth objective—a new world order—can emerge: a new era, freer from the threat of terror, stronger in the pursuit of justice, and more secure in the quest for peace. An era in which the nations of the world, east and west, north and south, can prosper and live in harmony.
>
> A hundred generations have searched for this elusive path to peace, while a thousand wars raged across the span of human endeavor. Today that new world is struggling to be born. A world quite different from the one we've known. A world in which the rule of law supplants the rule of the jungle.

A hundred generations. Let's see, that gets us back to the era of Abraham or thereabouts, in the days when Egypt rocked the cradle of civilization. From Egypt until 1990, no one had found the solution, not even Jesus Christ. I think Mr. Bush meant every word, as messianic as his extended timetable may initially appear. I have not seen this messianic a statement by any other major Western leader in my lifetime. But Mr. Bush learned a lesson in November of 1992: "Pride goeth before destruction, and an haughty spirit before a fall" (Proverbs 16:18).

There have been many conspiracies in history. A few gain power for a while; most of them lose from the beginning. These conspiracies have a model: the satanic conspiracy against God. They rely on secrecy covered in a shell of public positioning. They promote hidden agendas. They all lose. One by one, they all lose. This is why Isaiah warned God's people:

> You are not to say, "It is a conspiracy!" In regard to all that this people call a conspiracy, and you are not to fear what they fear or be in dread of it. It is the LORD of hosts whom you should regard as holy. And He shall be your fear, And he shall be your dread (Isa. 8:12–13, NASB).

H. G. Wells' legacy has come to naught. He is remembered today mainly as an early science fiction writer: *The War of the Worlds* and *The Time Machine*. His open conspiracy is still working to extend its New World Order, but it, too, will come to naught. Those who become paralyzed in fear just thinking about the success of this or that conspiracy have disobeyed Isaiah. Those who seek to discover the inner ring that runs all of the other conspiracies have adopted the worldview of the conspirators. There is no inner ring that controls them all— not an earthly inner ring, anyway. Readers must understand that the enemy can enmesh good people in his own web of impotence and fear by making them into conspiracy-hunters, conspiracy-exposers, and conspiracy-believers. I have known several very conservative people whose lives and careers have been destroyed pursuing the ultimate conspiracy.

Most historians have substituted some variation of cosmic impersonalism—the rule of impersonal forces—for the biblical concept of cosmic personalism: the rule of God. Conspiracy historians have usually substituted a rival version of cosmic personalism: the rule of secret societies. The thesis is the same, from the IBC (international bankers' conspiracy) to the IJBC (international Jewish bankers; conspiracy) to the Iluminati: the insiders have taken control of the key resource, whether money, the media, or whatever. This places the key to history inside history. It divinizes the relative.

There are limits to the imagination of man, but not many. The farthest reach of the limits of conspiracy historiography that I have ever come across is a 115-page book by one James Wood Monk: *Karl and Taffy* (1958), published by something called the Eldorado Pilgrim Press, Mountains of the Moon. On page 9, he announces his unique thesis. "This book is dedicated to the thesis that the most powerful nation in the world today is Wales, whose rate of multiplication and climb to power in at least five continents since 1485 has been little short of phenomenal." The year 1485 marked the defeat of Richard III by Henry Tudor of Wales.[11] If you think that the secret powers behind Western governments have been obscure, consider this one-sentence assessment: "This book seeks to stretch in outline the process whereby a combination of the faithless South Welsh who abandoned and the loyal North Welsh who supported the last Llywelyn of Wales in 1282 has [*sic*] now gained mastery of the island, and through it of the Empire, and through the Empire seeks to ally with British and Israelite forces in the United States to dominate the world in collusion with representatives of the original Marxist revolutionaries who assisted World Communism in its march to power" (p. 10). There are many hidden trails on the road to historiographical nuttiness, and Mr. Monk has done yeoman service in blazing one of them. A word to the wise is sufficient.

---

11. I was at Bosworth Field, where the battle took place, on its 500th anniversary. A few hundred visitors were there for the preliminaries to the weekend's reenactment of the battle. The followers of Richard III seemed to outnumber Henry's advocates. One of them cried out: "Death to the Welsh pretender!" Too late by 500 years, according to Mr. Monk.

INTRODUCTION

The high priest then asked Jesus of his disciples, and of his doctrine. Jesus answered him, I spake openly to the world; I ever taught in the synagogue, and in the temple, whither Jews always resort; and in secret have I said nothing. Why askest thou me? Ask them which heard me, what I have said unto them: behold, they know what I said (John 18:19–21).

A war is in progress. It is a war between light and darkness, truth and falsehood, ethics and power. It is also a war between two conflicting strategies: visible proclamation vs. secret organization, public representation vs. secret initiation. This war has been going on from the beginning (or at least one week after the beginning). It has been going on in human history since the serpent tempted Eve.

The public is blissfully unaware of the nature of this war. It is likely that most people will remain unaware of it in our lifetimes. But an increasing minority of people are becoming at least vaguely aware of what is going on. Nobody has all the answers—nobody on earth, anyway—but millions of people have heard at least part of the story. This book is an attempt to put the major issues in front of serious readers, especially Christian readers. I think there is finally a market for a little introductory book like this.

Open vs. Secret Ministries

Jesus' answer to the Pharisees proclaimed a fundamental principle of biblical organization: *the open ministry*. Jesus presented His whole message publicly. He spoke in parables, of course, but these only illustrated general principles. The parables did not establish some sort of secret conspiracy. He gave His disciples no program of secret initiation, no recruiting system based on something other than profession of faith in Christ and service to others. His told His opponents that they would be wasting their time to go hunting for secret messages or hidden codes in His public proclamations. Every principle in His message came from the Old Testament, which was a public document in Israel.

This organizational principle places the church in opposition to numerous secret societies. Jesus admonished His listeners:

> Ye are the light of the world. A city that is set on an hill cannot be hid. Neither do men light a candle, and put it under a bushel, but on a candlestick; and it giveth light unto all that are in the house. Let your light so shine before men, that they may see your good works, and glorify your Father which is in heaven (Matthew 5:14–16).

This principle of "open covenants openly arrived at" is basic to the history of Western Civilization. It is basic to all constitutionalism. The idea that the way to gain influence is by secret manipulation and hidden agendas is foreign to the Bible. What men are to do is to bring other men openly and publicly under God's four covenants: personal, church, family, state. Not by secret initiation but by public baptism; not by hidden sacrifices but by Christ's public sacrifice on the cross and by our public communion (the Lord's Supper) are we to exercise dominion.

But if this is God's way, then what of the enemies of God? What is their way? This book serves as an introductory answer to this fundamental organizational and historical question. But until we can agree on what, exactly, is the Bible's approach to a proper understanding of history, we remain be confused. People are not agreed about the nature of God, man, law, sanctions, and time.[1] Therefore, people are not agreed about the nature of history.

We need to be clear about this: the war I spoke of is also a war over the proper interpretation of historical facts. The facts don't just "speak for themselves." Men speak in the name of the facts they have chosen to speak about. We are creatures. We are not omniscient. Therefore, we all pick and choose the facts that we believe are most relevant. *Relevant to whose purposes and relevant to what goals?* Therein lies the problem of historical interpretation.

The Public's Skepticism

Over the last 30 years, and especially since 1971, there has been an increasing interest in the United States concerning the existence, influence, and relevance of hidden, clandestine conspiracies. All ideological groups have participated. We have been presented with numerous "conspiracy theories" from the conservative right,[2] the libertarian right,[3] the old left (which generally prefers "power groupings" or "class influence" to more highly personalized conspiracy theories),[4] and the new

---

1. Ray R. Sutton, *That You May Prosper: Dominion By Covenant* (2nd ed.; Tyler, Texas: Institute for Christian Economics, 1992).

2. The classic example is the book by Gary Allen and Larry Abraham, *None Dare Call It Conspiracy* (1972) and the sequel by Abraham, *Call It Conspiracy* (1985).

3. The works of Antony Sutton are the best examples: see the Bibliography. Murray Rothbard's book, *America's Great Depression* (Princeton: Van Nostrand, 1963), is a conspiracy theory of the origins of the great depression in the pro-British inflationary monetary policies of the Coolidge era and the statist responses of Herbert Hoover. See also Rothbard, *Wall Street, Banks, and American Foreign Policy* (Burlingame, California: RRR, 1995); *The Case Against the Fed* (Auburn, Alabama: Ludwig von Mises Institute, 1994).

4. A best-seller of the late 1960's was Ferdinand Lundberg, *The Rich and the Super-Rich: A Study in the Power of Money* (New York: Lyle Stuart, 1968). For a more scholarly sociological analysis, see G. William Donhoff, *Who Rules America Now? A View*

left.[5] If any single event was most responsible for this growing interest, it was the assassination of President John F. Kennedy on November 22, 1963. A wave of books on the Kennedy assassination has appeared, from Mark Lane's *Rush to Judgment* (1966) to David Lifton's *Best Evidence* (1980). One scholarly bibliography, published in 1980, listed over 5,000 sources on the subject.[6] By now there are probably thousands more.

The conclusion of the Warren Commission's report on the assassination—Lee Harvey Oswald was a lone killer without any institutional connections—was predictable. He was just a mixed-up fellow. He was a "nut." This has been the official coin of the realm in every post-assassination investigation, from Garfield and McKinley to the Kennedys, from Martin Luther King to George Wallace (who at least survived the ordeal). "The Lone Assassin, mentally disturbed, strikes again." And anyone who doesn't believe this explanation, it is implied by establishment commentators, scholars, and official spokesmen, is himself mentally disturbed. But one thing is sure: when it comes to *this* form of "mental disturbance," the mentally disturbed person is hardly alone. Things have changed since November 22, 1963— to a great extent, *because* of November 22, 1963.

The generally skeptical or at least unenthusiastic response of American readers (a minority of Americans) to the Warren Commission's report was not predictable back in 1964, when the Committee began its work. This skepticism startled the Establishment. So has its aftermath. Skepticism by the American

---

for the '80s (New York: Prentice Hall, 1983). It is not a blatantly ideological book. The most detailed study ever written on this topic is Philip H. Burch's *Elites in American History*, 3 vols. (New York: Holmes & Meier, 1980).

5. Holly Sklar (ed.), *Trilateralism: The Trilateral Commission and Elite Planning for World Management* (P. O. Box 68, Astor Station, Boston, Massachusetts: South End Press, 1980); Kees van der Pijl, *The Making of an Atlantic Ruling Class* (London: Verso, 1984). Both publishers are quite obscure.

6. Lloyd J. Guth and David R. Wrone, *The Assassination of John F. Kennedy: A Comprehensive Historical and Legal Bibliography, 1963–1979* (Westport, Connecticut: Greenwood Press, 1980).

public concerning anything the government announces officially has increased exponentially over the last three decades. It has affected every realm of life. It has affected every academic discipline.[7]

This skepticism has unquestionably had effects in the area of historical explanation. Americans have developed a real taste for odd-ball explanations of any and every historic event. Books have appeared that seek to prove that: Butch Cassidy wasn't killed in South America; some of the Czar's family were rescued in 1918; John Dillinger wasn't killed by the FBI; Amelia Earhart didn't crash, and the plane she was supposed to be flying turned up decades later in at an auction; Sacco and Vanzetti didn't kill anyone (or maybe Sacco did but Vanzetti didn't); Bruno Hauptman didn't kidnap the Lindbergh baby; Roosevelt knew the Japanese were about to attack Pearl Harbor; Hitler didn't liquidate the Jews; Dwight D. Eisenhower was a conscious agent of the Communist conspiracy, implying therefore, even more improbably (in the opinion of many), that Dwight D. Eisenhower was conscious; the United States is controlled by a secret conspiracy of: 1) Jewish bankers; 2) Freemasons; 3) the Illuminati; 4) the Council on Foreign Relations; 5) the Trilateral Commission; 6) monopoly capitalists; 7) Communist agents; 8) the Vatican; 9) Theosophists; 10) British bankers who are behind the world's drug smugglers and who are in fact agents of the Queen; 11) a cult of mystic Masters who were trained in Tibet; 12) visitors from outer space who have taken on human characteristics; 13) four of the above; 14) all of the above. And we dare not forget that perennial favorite: "The Rosenbergs were framed!"

About the only thesis that has not been offered so far is that Nixon really didn't know anything about the Watergate break-in until he read about it in the *Washington Post*.

---

7. Gary North, "The Crisis of American Universities," in North (ed.), *Foundations of Christian Scholarship* (Vallecito, California: Ross House Books, 1976).

Then comes the inevitable question: *Who is covering up?* And why? Why the *conspiracy of silence?*

Is all of this crazy? Or is some of it correct? What should the serious Christian think about conspiracies? This little book is designed to help you come to Bible-based conclusions concerning these questions.

1

THE REALITY OF CONSPIRACIES

Why do the heathen rage, and the people imagine a vain thing? The kings of the earth set themselves, and the rulers take counsel together, against the LORD, and against his anointed, saying, "Let us break their bands asunder, and cast away their cords from us." He that sitteth in the heavens shall laugh: the LORD shall hold them in derision. Then shall he speak unto them in wrath, and vex them in his sore displeasure (Psalm 2:1–5).

People from time to time ask me what I think of the conspiracy view of history. My answer is usually not what they expect, whether they are pro-conspiracy theorists or anti-conspiracy theorists.

Why do they bother to ask me? Probably because they have spotted my weak point: a near-maniacal addiction to history books. By training, I'm an historian. I even have a Ph.D. in the field. This means that I had three choices when I got out of school: go into teaching and starve, stay out of teaching and starve, or go into business and not starve (maybe). I did the latter, and I haven't starved (so far). But I still read a lot of history books. I just can't stop.

I have a theory of history. It begins with Genesis 1:1: God's creation of the universe out of nothing.

Cosmic Personalism

You need to understand something about serious Christians and serious Jews: they have a view of history which is *personal*. They recognize that God created the world. The world is not now, nor has it ever been, an impersonal product of random material forces. Biblical religion is inescapably a religion of *cosmic personalism*.[1] Men are responsible personal agents—responsible primarily to God and secondarily to each other through institutional arrangements: church, State, family, economy. (I capitalize "State" when I refer to civil government in general; I don't capitalize it when I refer to the regional legal jurisdiction known as a "state.") Furthermore, biblical religion sees history as the product of a giant cosmic struggle: between good and evil, between God and Satan, between redeemed men and rebellious men. This struggle is innately and inescapably *personal*.

This struggle is not simply personal, however; it is inherently *conspiratorial*. The Bible tells about a great conspiracy against God. It is a conspiracy which affects every area of life, including politics. David describes it in Psalm 2. In David's day, there was a conspiracy among the kings of the earth against God. It was in existence long before David's day. That same conspiracy is still raging, even though there are no more kings of any importance left on earth.[2] It is an age-old struggle.

For as long as there are history and sin, members of this conspiracy will be enraged at righteousness. The conspirators "breathe together" (*con* = with; *spire* = breathe). They "breathe together" against God and God's law, and also against all those who are faithful to God, or who may not even believe in God,

---

1. Gary North, *The Dominion Covenant: Genesis* (2nd ed.; Tyler, Texas: Institute for Christian Economics, 1987), ch. 1: "Cosmic Personalism."

2. King Farouk, the deposed puppet monarch of Egypt, put it very well when he announced: "There are but five kings left in the world: the king of England, and the kings of clubs, diamonds, spades, and hearts."

but who are faithful to God's precepts. Western Civilization's moral foundations and especially legal foundations were constructed in terms of biblical morality and biblical law.[3] Thus, *the conspirators are at war against Western Civilization.* It outrages them.

C. S. Lewis

No one has described their outrage more graphically than the English Christian scholar and novelist, C. S. Lewis, in his magnificent novel, *That Hideous Strength* (1945). It is the third novel in his "space trilogy," and it is by far the most important. In this novel, Lewis creates a "fantasy" about a government-funded scientific research organization (N.I.C.E.) which is hierarchically controlled by systematically evil men who intend to suppress the liberties of the whole population. These men are part of a conspiracy. They have adopted the traditional organizational structure of occultism: secrecy, inner rings of authority, initiation, and a false front of benevolence for the public to believe in. They seek power with a vengeance, including occult magical power.

Lewis understood that rationalism and materialism can be combined with magic. This was a remarkable insight. That he understood it in the 1940's is astounding. He was virtually alone in this belief then. Events since 1965 have shown how correct he was. Occultism has been on the rise, especially on university campuses.[4]

(Lewis, oddly enough, died on November 22, 1963, the same day that President John F. Kennedy died, and the same day that English novelist-atheist Aldous Huxley died. It was Huxley's grandfather, Thomas Huxley, who first promoted and popularized Charles Darwin's *Origin of Species* [1859], which has

---

3. Harold J. Berman, *Law and Revolution: The Formation of the Western Legal Tradition* (Cambridge, Massachusetts: Harvard University Press, 1983).

4. Gary North, *Unholy Spirits: New Age Humanism and Occultism* (Tyler, Texas: Institute for Christian Economics, [1986] 1994).

probably been the most important book in the arsenal of the conspiracy—vastly more important, at least in the industrialized West, than anything written by Karl Marx, another dedicated follower of Darwin.[5])

The Establishment's Conspiracy

I want to make one thing perfectly clear (as Richard Nixon used to say): everyone believes in the existence of conspiracies. Conspiracies are organized groups of people who maliciously plot to undermine whatever it is you believe in. Obviously, what you believe in is good, so they are evil. Since there are always fringe groups who have not yet "seen the light," and who plot against goodness and true justice, those who believe in good-ness and true justice need to defend themselves by stamping out (or at least exposing) these illegal groups. These groups are clearly illegal, since good and just people get their rulers to pass laws making such conspiracies illegal. In short, as the Christian scholar R. J. Rushdoony has written, "The commonly admitted conspiracies are those of the opposition."[6]

There is nothing remarkable in all this. Clearly, it isn't worth a whole book. But what the more recent conspiracy thesis books argue, especially *None Dare Call It Conspiracy* (1972) and its sequel, *Call It Conspiracy* (1985),[7] is that not only are there con-spiracies, but that there is *one major conspiracy* in the twen-tieth-century, and that this conspiracy has actually succeeded in capturing the major institutions of modern society: church,

---

5. Marx wrote to Ferdinand Lassalle in early 1861: "Darwin's book is very important and serves me as a basis in natural science for the class struggle in histo-ry." Karl Marx and Friederich Engels, *Correspondence, 1846-1895*, edited by Dona Torr (New York: International Publishers, 1935), p. 125. He had written to Engels a few weeks earlier: ". . . this is the book which contains the basis in natural history for our view." *Ibid.*, p. 126.

6. R. J. Rushdoony, *The Nature of the American System* (Fairfax, Virginia: Thoburn Press, [1965] 1978), p. 143.

7. Larry Abraham, *Call It Conspiracy* (Seattle, Washington: Double A Publications, 1985).

State, the media, big business organizations, the prestigious universities, and the banking establishment. Above all, the banking establishment.

Establishment: this is the key word. The oddity of the thesis lies here: the conspiracy *is* the Establishment. It is not like the conspiracy of the Bolsheviks against the Czar's establishment. Everyone understands that sort of conspiracy: a rag-tag band of vicious outsiders who plot to capture the seats of authoritarian power for themselves. No, what we are facing is a successful conspiracy of the American Establishment against the Constitution of the United States and against everyone who was intended by the Constitution's authors to be protected by that Constitution. Operationally speaking, there is a secret constitution in the shadow of the official one, and the elite governs in terms of it.[8] This is a conspiracy of insiders against outsiders, not the other way around. It is a conspiracy of super-rich and super-powerful insiders who quietly captured the seats of power *in the name of the "true outsiders," the downtrodden masses.* It is a conspiracy of the well-connected against the disorganized and disconnected. In other words, there are conspiracies, and then there are *Conspiracies*!

The Lone Assassin

Anyone who accepts the existence of such a conspiracy is written off (by whom?) either as a fool or a rogue. Let me offer an example. I have said in the introduction that the interest in conspiracies has been fueled by the question of who shot President Kennedy. I have said that the "lone assassin" theory is the only acceptable theory in "official" circles.

There are always some post-assassination questions that must be raised. Here are four that the public wants answered, and

---

8. Arthur S. Miller, *The Secret Constitution and the Need for Constitutional Change* (Westport, Connecticut: Greenwood, 1987).

therefore the official board of inquiry attempts to provide answers for:

> Who shot him?
> Why did this man say that he shot him?
> Was he acting alone?
> What were the man's previous actions?

Everyone knows that all assassins are madmen who act alone. Everyone knows this, even when the evidence points to other conclusions. The Establishment's committee-approved interpretations of every presidential assassin except John Wilkes Booth invariably conclude this. The "kooks" claim otherwise. Who is a "kook"? Anyone who claims otherwise.

Why is this the standard interpretation? For a conspiracy to have successfully replaced the highest political figure in the land would raise too many questions. If the assassin did not act by himself, people might start asking additional questions, such as:

> Who financed him?
> What did his financiers expect to gain?
> Who replaced the President in office?
> Who has gained what from the new man?
> Is the public at the mercy of murderers?
> Should they, too, be investigated?

In the case of John Wilkes Booth, historians do admit that this was a conspiracy. We know that several boarders at Mary Surratt's boarding house were involved. After all, one of them tried to kill Secretary of State Seward the same night. So there was a conspiracy—*a conspiracy of nonentities*. Then, in 1937, an amateur historian (what else?) named Otto Eisenschiml had his book published, *Why Was Lincoln Murdered?*, a book which presents evidence that points to Stanton, Lincoln's Secretary of War, and other anti-Lincoln Radical Republicans as very possibly involved. This book is no longer in print, despite the fact that books on Lincoln seem to sell forever. This is not the sort of conspiracy which is discussed in college classrooms in U.S. history—or any other history. This may have been a conspiracy of "Insiders."

A Quiet Revolution

Rushdoony remarked in 1965 that "The successful and continuing conspiracies of history are never admitted to be conspiracies. Their known activities are extolled as virtues and patriotic works, never as illicit activities. Legitimacy is the reward of success, and only that which is seemly is admitted as acceptable party history."[9]

The offense of Gary Allen and Larry Abraham's book, *None Dare Call It Conspiracy* (1972, 4.5 million sold), and W. Cleon Skousen's *The Naked Capitalist* (1970, a million sold) is that they argued that America's present rulers are the organizational and spiritual heirs of a band of bloodless revolutionaries who pulled off a true revolution in the United States, though a nearly invisible revolution, in the early decades of this century.

On the surface, the thesis sounds absolutely crazy. A revolution without an uprising? A revolution without manifestos? But wouldn't this be the best possible sort of revolution from the point of view of the revolutionaries? A revolution which sounds crazy to its victims, even seven decades after it took place?

But what if it had a manifesto? What if the senior advisor to the President who launched the somewhat more visible phase of the revolution had written it? What about *Philip Drew, Administrator* (1912), the anonymous novel by "Col." Edward Mandel House, Wilson's alter ego?[10] It featured a hero who takes over the government and imposes a new order on society. Don't ask.

---

9. Rushdoony, *Nature of the American System*, p. 142.

10. On House's authorship, see *The Intimate Papers of Colonel House*, edited by Charles Seymour, 4 vols. (Boston: Houghton Mifflin, 1926), I, p. 152.

And if you ask, don't expect a straight answer from a professional historian.

Setting the Agenda

Here is the offending thesis: through their domination over the major educational, political, and financial institutions, these conspirators have "set the agenda," especially the *intellectual* agenda, for the last century. The kinds of questions they want asked are the only kinds of questions that wise (and *prudent*) men do ask. The kinds of answers that they want investigators to come up with are the only kinds of answers that wise (and *prudent*) men do come up with. In short, they have established that elusive but powerful "climate of opinion" which governs the affairs of men.

Elsewhere, I have called this process "capturing the robes."[11] Those institutions in Western Civilization that have been marked by robes—the clergy, the judiciary, and university professors—were targeted a century ago by conspiratorial groups. These groups did everything they could to capture the leadership of each group, in order to mold public opinion. They have been remarkably successful in their efforts.

We might also call this process "capturing the *minds*." It is incorrect to say that a man is what he eats. It is also incorrect to say that a man is what he owns. No, a man is what he *thinks*, what he truly believes in. Shape his thinking, and you can manipulate the man. Shape the thinking of *the spokesmen of the activist minority* in any society, and you can manipulate that society (within shifting limits historically, of course). Political or financial control over institutions is not enough. Temporary political power is not enough. You can eventually lose control to other dedicated conspiratorial groups. Therefore, control over people's access to information, and more importantly,

---

11. Gary North, *Backward, Christian Soldiers?* (Tyler, Texas: Institute for Christian Economics, 1984), ch. 7.

control over *the moral and theoretical principles that govern their interpretation of information*, is essential. Lose this, and you have in principle lost control. You *will* eventually lose control. No civilization has ever fallen to outsiders that did not first suffer a loss of faith in its first principles. *The failure of faith always precedes the failure of will.*[12]

In the United States, the conspirators understood the nature of the conflict from the time of the Abolitionist movement.[13] Consider the career of Rev. Thomas Wentworth Higgenson, a Unitarian minister. He once wrote a letter to the murderous John Brown in which he announced: "I am always ready to invest money in treason. . . ."[14] Higgenson had a long and perverse career. He was an active supporter of Horace Mann's Massachusetts experiment in state-supported public education, a member of the Secret Six which financed John Brown in the 1850's, and a founder of the Intercollegiate Society of Socialists in 1905, along with Clarence Darrow, Jack London, Upton Sinclair, and others.[15] The I.S.S. later became known as the League for Industrial Democracy, a first cousin (or closer) of the British Fabian socialist society.[16]

These sorts of men, and others far richer and with more capital to defend, saw to it that they and their allies gained control of those institutions that can legally sound the alarm against any infringement of the people's Constitutional liberties: the courts (especially the Supreme Court), the Congress, and the Executive (especially the Cabinet). Also, they captured the institutions that teach and inform the people who generally

---

12. Gilbert Murray, *The Five Stages of Greek Religion* (Garden City, New York: Doubleday Anchor, [1925]).

13. Otto Scott, *The Secret Six: John Brown and the Abolitionist Movement* (New York: Times Books, 1979).

14. Cited by J. C. Furnas, *The Road to Harper's Ferry* (New York: William Sloane, 1959), p. 337.

15. Rushdoony, *Nature of the American System*, p. 19n.

16. Rose L. Martin, *Fabian Freeway: High Road to Socialism in the U.S.A.* (Boston: Western Islands, 1966), pp. 191–92.

become the senior decision-makers in society: the media (the three major T.V. networks and the major journals of opinion), the major book publishing firms, the public schools, and most importantly, Harvard, Princeton, Yale, Chicago, Berkeley, Michigan, and the other prestigious universities.

Interpreting the U.S. Constitution

What the conspirators have done is to short-circuit the true meaning, and true limitations on the Federal government, of the U.S. Constitution. They have nationalized and centralized a political order which was deliberately created to be a decentralized system. As Professor Miller has described in detail, they have in effect substituted a secret constitution for the official one.

Most people are afraid of calling attention to this capture of power, for in doing so, *they would themselves become targets of the accusation that they had become "treasonous" or "conspiratorial"*—conspirators against those who seem to be able to announce the standards of goodness and true justice. In short, the success of the conspirators can be seen in their ability to make their critics look like conspirators. Or fools. "You mean you think that the U.S. Supreme Court doesn't understand the Constitution, and you do? Why, you must be crazy!" Who wants to appear crazy?

And yet, and yet. . . . More and more people have looked at the decisions of the Supreme Court—on compulsory busing of public school children, on striking down state laws against abortion, on the insanity defense which allows someone to shoot the President of the United States and escape prison—and they have concluded, "The Supreme Court is crazy, not me."

This shift of thinking, above all else, is what the conspiracy fears. It is a shift in the "climate of opinion." It is a shift which they find difficult to control any longer, and which threatens their monopoly of influence. This shift has taken place since 1970.

The offense of pages 936–956 of Prof. Carroll Quigley's *Tragedy and Hope* (Macmillan, 1966), *None Dare Call It Conspiracy*, and similar conspiracy thesis books, is found in the thesis that a dedicated conspiracy has quietly captured the power centers in order to further its own ends against. . . . Against what?

To identify a conspiracy, you must also identify the "conspired against." The identification of the "conspired against" establishes which kind of conspiracy thesis the author is promoting. There are Marxist-written conspiracy books that criticize the Rockefeller interests as pro-capitalist. There are "right-wing" conspiracy theses that are anti-Rockefeller because of the State capitalism aspect of the Establishment. Usually, the focus of concern is on politics and/or economic monopoly. Very seldom is the conspiracy traced back farther than two centuries, with the exception of anti-Semitic conspiracy theses, and even these generally begin with the Rothschild family in the late 18th century.

The Biblical View

The Bible reveals a much longer conspiratorial time frame: a continuing conspiracy against God and His revealed law-order. The faces change, but the issue remains the same: *ethics.* Money, power, prestige, and influence all flow out of this fundamental issue: *Which God should men worship?* As the prophet Elijah presented the issue before the people of Israel when they gathered on Mt. Carmel during the reign of Israel's evil king, Ahab: "How long halt ye between two opinions? If the Lord be God, follow him; but if Baal, then follow him." The next sentence is most revealing: "And the people answered him not a word" (I Kings 18:21). They never do, until they see who is going to win the confrontation.

The biblical view of conspiracy neither overestimates the power of conspiracies nor underestimates it. There is one conspiracy, Satan's, and ultimately it must fail. Satan's supernatural conspiracy is *the* conspiracy; all other visible conspiracies are merely outworkings of this supernatural conspiracy. This is the testimony of the whole Bible, from Genesis to Revelation. The Bible's account of the Tower of Babel records one unsuccessful effort of the conspiracy, and it ended in the defeat of the conspirators. The cross of Calvary is the ultimate example: satanically successful on the surface, but it led within three days to the definitive defeat in principle of Satan and his host. Christ's resurrection definitively smashed in principle the satanic conspiracy. History since Calvary is simply the outworking of that definitive victory.

The one overarching conspiracy is therefore in principle *disunited*. "He that is not with me is against me," Jesus said, "and he that gathereth not with me scattereth abroad" (Matthew 12:30). This was the conclusion in a line of reasoning which began when the Pharisees criticized Jesus for having exorcised demons. He did it, they argued, by the power of Satan. Jesus knew their thoughts, and He replied: "Every kingdom divided against itself is brought to desolation; and every city or house divided against itself shall not stand. And if Satan cast out Satan, he is divided against himself; how then shall his kingdom stand?" (Matthew 12:25–26).

This is the biblical view of the conspiracy of Satan against God: Satan has power even to exorcise his own followers, the demons, but this very power points to his divided kingdom and his coming defeat. He can divide his own earthly followers, engaging them in endless wars, so great is his hatred of mankind, but he cannot defeat God and God's covenantally faithful people.

There is a surface unity among the conspirators: unity against the enemy, God. This illusion of unity has confused many Christians and almost all conspiracy theorists. Nevertheless, the conspirators understand each other. They distrust each other, for they know how ready and willing one subgroup is to subvert and overturn the plans of a rival group. When they forget this lesson, they pay the price. Stalin is a good example.

Despite continual warnings from his spies and military advisors, he trusted Hitler right up until the day that the Nazis invaded the Soviet Union in June of 1941. From that time on, Stalin's paranoia increased exponentially (and it had always been high). He never trusted anyone again. Why should he? All those around him were miniature dictators. Like he had always been, they were conspirators. There was no one worth his trust.

Try building a long-term civilization on paranoia. It cannot be done. The power religion eventually collapses. There is no honor among thieves; there is only suspicion. In the long run, conspiracies against God and His law must fail.

2

THE PEOPLE'S WILL

And Absalom sent for Ahithophel the Gilonite, David's counsellor, from his city, even from Giloh, while he offered sacrifices. And the conspiracy was strong; for the people increased continually with Absalom. And there came a messenger to David, saying, The hearts of the men of Israel are after Absalom (II Samuel 15:12–13).

David was the lawful king of Israel. He had been anointed by Samuel, called by his people, and victorious on the battlefield. He had consistently refused to take up the sword against Saul, even after Samuel had anointed David. He was content to wait for God to demonstrate through historical circumstances that David was the lawful king. He had never been involved in a premature grabbing of the robes of political authority. God eventually delivered the kingdom into his hand.

David had at least eight wives and many sons. The line of succession to the throne was in doubt. This did not please Absalom. Like all revolutionaries, he was impatient to wear the robes of authority. He had already had his equally evil brother Amnon murdered (II Samuel 13:28–29). Now he plotted a conspiracy to overthrow David, capture the throne, and eliminate his family rivals. He pretended to be a friend of the people and a friend of righteous judgment (II Samuel 15:2–6). The

Bible records, "so Absalom stole the hearts of the men of Israel (v. 6). The people's hearts were easily stolen. Things have not changed. Absalom's rebellion led to civil war. He came very close to achieving his goal.

The Bible calls this action of Absalom and the people a conspiracy. The Hebrew word can also be translated as "treason." What this teaches us is that the people are not sovereign. God is sovereign, and His law is sovereign. The Bible does not teach "vox populi, vox dei" (the voice of the people is the voice of God). When the people of a society accept the idea that the people's will is absolutely sovereign, they thereby condemn themselves to a life of manipulation by corrupt elites that will seek to rule "in the name of the People." They have condemned themselves to a political order of rigged elections, "plebiscites," and 99% majority voting for one-party dictatorships.

Representation

The biblical doctrine of human leadership is the doctrine of representation.[1] The leader is to represent God to the people and the people to God.[2] Like the Old Testament priest who offered sacrifices to God for the people, so are the head of the household, the political ruler, and the church leader supposed to enforce righteous laws for the people (Romans 13:1–7). Each has specific laws which he is supposed to enforce, but all three offices are to be governed by God's law—God's principles of righteous judgment.

All political rule is founded on a doctrine of representation. This is an inescapable concept. It is never a question of "representation vs. no representation." It is always a question of *whose*

---

1. Ray R. Sutton, *That You May Prosper: Dominion By Covenant* (2nd ed.; Tyler, Texas: Institute for Christian Economics, 1992), ch. 2.

2. Gary North, *Leviticus: An Economic Commentary* (Tyler, Texas: Institute for Christian Economics, 1994), ch. 4.

representation? Which officer lawfully represents which group
of people in what specified capacity before which sovereign
lord? Until men understand and accept this biblical view of
government—self-government, family government, church government, and civil government—they will be tossed to and fro
by the conflicting winds of rebellious opinion.

God does not lodge absolute sovereignty in any human
institution. Men are sinners, and no single institution can safely
be entrusted with absolute sovereignty. Absolute power would
corrupt sinful men if it were available, but it isn't. Nevertheless,
some men seek it, and this search is a sign of their corruption
and a means of corrupting them further.

The point is, conspiracies really do exist. People conspire
together to achieve evil ends. We use the word to describe a
confederacy which is set up for illegal or immoral ends. It is a
confederation which aims at capturing power but without legitimate authorization by God or other God-ordained, lawful institutions. (The American Revolution was justified by its proponents by means of constitutional arguments. Congress was seen
by them as a lawful confederation of lawfully ordained local
state assemblies against a British Parliament which was illegally
centralizing power and against a king who had capitulated to
Parliament and who was therefore in a conspiracy against the
colonial assemblies and traditional common law liberties.)[3]

Anti-Conspiracy Theories

There are numerous "establishment" theories that are used
by conventional historians to explain the past: technological
determinism, psychological determinism, economic determinism, geographical determinism, and random indeterminism. To
this, add political history, military history, population history,
the history of ideas, and too many other subfields to mention,

---

3. R. J. Rushdoony, *This Independent Republic: Studies in the Nature and Meaning of
American History* (Fairfax, Virginia: Thoburn Press, [1964] 1978), chaps. 2, 3.

let alone summarize. But in this century—indeed, since Rousseau's late 18th-century writings—one view seems to prevail, at least in the history textbooks: *the will of the People.*

The concept of "the People" has, for over a century, served the "toreadors" of professional historiography as a red cape: to focus the attention of the victims away from the sword. The People's will cannot be thwarted, we all know. Watch the People march forward! The People will control the evil special-interest groups. Federal legislation will protect the People, for the People have so willed it. Forget about actual individuals; keep your eyes on the People.

Does all this sound vaguely familiar? We can almost see Dorothy in front of the screen, with the Wizard's glaring face looking out at her. "Don't mess with the People! The People's will is sovereign!" she is warned. Meanwhile, Toto is behind the curtain, pulling at an old man's pants leg. "Pay no attention to the old man behind the curtain," she is sternly warned by the image.

There are some people behind that curtain who don't want you to pay any attention, and they are not "the People." They've even gone to the expense of training and employing three generations of professional historians to explain to you why nothing important is going on back there.

Naive Conservatives

The problem is, too many conspiracy theorists naively believe in a conservative version of the will of the People. They understand that the People do not, in fact, understand what is going on, and that the People do not control the drift of events. Nevertheless, these theorists believe that if the People really did understand what is going on and has gone on, they would "take matters into their own hands." They would rise up and throw off their chains. In other words, the world *should* be governed by the People. The world *could* be governed by the

People. It is just that somehow the world isn't governed by the People.

What we need, therefore, is a successful exposé of the conspirators. If enough Americans (or whoever) could just learn about their unelected masters, they would no longer tolerate such a state of affairs. Such a theory of history rests on a presupposition that men can be saved by knowledge. If men just *knew* what has taken place, they would reassert their lawful sovereignty over the affairs of men. They would vote in the "right" people. They would throw out the "bums." Thus, we must devote ourselves to a mass-based program of exposure. This, in and of itself, will bring the People to their senses.

Samuel's Warning

God knew better. When He instructed the prophet Samuel to warn the people of Israel against establishing a king—that is, warn them against establishing a king other than the Lord—He knew that they would not heed the warning. Why not? Because their hearts were evil. They had become rebels against God; they did not want Him to rule over them any longer (I Samuel 8:7). So Samuel described the taxes, wars, and confiscation to come. Sure enough: they refused to listen.

So he warned them again: "And ye shall cry out in that day because of your king which ye shall have chosen you; and the Lord will not hear you in that day. Nevertheless the people refused to obey the voice of Samuel; and they said, Nay, but we will have a king rule over us; that we may be like other nations; and that our king may judge us, and go out before us, and fight our battles" (I Samuel 8:18–20).

The testimony of their long-time spiritual leader did not bring the people of Israel to repentance. They refused to listen. Then why should mere knowledge about and exposure of immoral and elitist leaders bring today's voters to their senses? The primary issues of life are *ethical*, not intellectual. They are primarily questions of right and wrong, not true and false—or, better put, the question of true and false *facts* cannot be dealt with successfully until men understand the difference between right and wrong *acts*. Until they are willing to choose right rather than wrong, all the facts in the world will not help them; the wide availability of facts will simply condemn them. From those to whom much is given, much is expected (Luke 12:48).

"Who shot President Kennedy?" is not the main issue. What *is* relevant is this question: What kind of society were President Kennedy and his advisors, his successor Lyndon Johnson and his advisors, and their rivals the Communists *really* trying to build? The answer is clear: societies that either ignore God or reject God. They were generally successful in their efforts. Worry therefore about God's response to national indifference; don't worry too much about assassins.

Salvation by Education?

Question: If a group (or allied groups) of ideologically linked, educationally linked, financially linked, and even maritally linked rulers do, in fact, control the basic policy-making of the U.S. government, along with big banking, big labor, big business, and big everything else, do they do so in defiance of what most Americans would want them to do, *if they knew who was controlling decision-making and how they were doing it*? If they really do exercise such power, then they are clearly unelected rulers. If American voters had the opportunity to vote for them and their policies, would the voters elect them? Or would the voters throw them out?

If you answer, "Most Americans would throw out the conspirators, if they only knew about them," you are saying that *you* would throw them out because *you* know about them, and you think other Americans would agree with you.

I'm not so sure that they would. I think the whole "Gang of 2300" (Council on Foreign Relations) should be tossed out into the cold, cruel world of economic competition. If I were President of the United States, no C.F.R. member or Trilateral Commission member could serve in any position subject to my appointment. But that isn't the point. I am not sure that the "average" American voter cares one way or the other. I doubt that I could gain many votes for President in terms of such a campaign promise, other than from those who have read the various little paperback books on conspiracy, even if the power elite were to stand on the sidelines and refuse to get involved in the election.

It is unquestionably my job to get involved in an educational campaign. That is what this little book is all about. I want to get leaders of the future to see the issues—the biblical issues and the Constitutional issues—and abide by the Constitution, or change it openly, according to the rules. I think that voters (or at least those who care enough to take leadership positions locally) can eventually be persuaded to return to Constitutional principles. I think it will take something like a spiritual revival to accomplish this, however (which I happen to believe is coming). I know that it is my responsibility to try to win them back. This is the key word: *back*. Back from apathy, back from compromise, and back from false interpretations of the Constitution that have led to the centralization of power.

The Moral High Ground

What I am saying is this: the vast majority of American and Western voters began changing their economic opinions a century ago, decades before there was a C.F.R. A fundamental moral shift took place simultaneously with the rise of the conspiratorial (or "proto-conspiratorial") groups. The more thoughtful elitists no doubt did what they could to accelerate this shift, but they could not have created it—not in a "bottom-up," decentralized society, which the United States still was. The shift came because of widespread changes in theology, philosophy, and morality in the late nineteenth century, especially in urban churches and in the better universities. I believe that the most important factor in that shift was the rise of theological liberalism (what later came to be called the social gospel) and the spread of Darwinism and other forms of evolutionistic thinking.[4] This moral shift led to the rise of the early twentieth-century American movement which historians call "Progressivism." The point is, it was part of a major shift in the climate of moral opinion, and no conspiratorial group created it. They did, however, use it and profit from it. They still do.

Take the case of the sixteenth amendment, the Federal income tax. (As an aside, Red Beckman and former Illinois revenue agent Bill Benson have discovered that it was never ratified properly in 1913. Technically, it is an illegal amendment.[5] Is this really significant, except as a curiosity of history? The 14th amendment wasn't ratified legally, either, since certain states were not allowed to vote. The point is, the public in 1913 was willing to ratify it, even though certain technicalities were missing. There was no hue and cry of outrage when the amendment was announced as having passed. Why not? Therein lies a tale.)

How was that amendment sold to American voters? By an exceedingly evil appeal: "Soak the rich!" It was an appeal based on covetousness, pure and simple. And, like all forms of evil, it backfired. It led to the capture of the middle-class voters by the rich who were supposedly the targets of the law.

Rockefeller, Harriman, Morgan, Carnegie, and all the other "masters of 1913" knew how to to recruit and control professional politicians, who in turn knew how appeal to the voters. The 16th amendment was a classic Brer Rabbit ploy: "Don't toss us into that briar patch! Anything but that." And poor, dumb middle-class voters acted just like Brer Fox. They tossed the elite into the briar patch—the briar patch of tax-exempt

---

4. C. Gregg Singer, *A Theological Interpretation of American History* (Nutley, New Jersey: Craig Press, 1964).

5. Bill Benson and M. J. 'Red' Beckman, *The Law That Never Was—The Fraud of the 16th Amendment and Personal Income Tax* (Box 550, South Holland, Illinois: Constitutional Research Associates, 1985).

foundations, tax loopholes, family trusts, and all the rest. The elite had the lawyers and accountants. The middle class didn't.

Liberal historian and social commentator John Brooks has described the process well:

> . . . when the founder of the Ford Motor Company and his son made their wills, they left 90 percent of their Ford stock to their private foundation rather than paying nearly all of it to the government in taxes, thereby making that foundation the richest charitable organization in the history of the world—and, incidentally, preserving family control of the motor company, and even relieving the heirs to the other 10 percent of the stock of the necessity of paying any inheritance taxes! The hard-shelled Henry Ford, who had lived beyond his time, must have gone to his grave in 1947 chortling over how he had beat the government out of his money and made philanthropy pay.[6]

John D. Rockefeller, Sr., did the same thing. Andrew Carnegie did, too, but for different reasons: he had only one heir and really didn't believe that rich people should leave much money to heirs anyway.[7] All three set up huge foundations, and they all became strategic institutions for the capture of influence. Liberals and left wing reformers were successful in capturing them.[8] In 1983, Henry Ford II resigned in disgust from the board of the Ford Foundation, announcing that it had become an institution of anti-capitalist opinion. He learned slowly; it had been that from the very beginning.

When conservatives finally caught on and began to do the same thing in the 1960's, Congress changed the rules (in 1969). Today it is impossible for super-rich conservatives (and there aren't many of them any more, now that oil prices have

---

6. John Brooks. *The Great Leap: The Past Twenty-Five Years in America* (New York: Harper & Row, 1966), p. 74.

7. Andrew Carnegie, *The Gospel of Wealth* (1889).

8. René Wormser, *Foundations: Their Power and Influence* (New York: Davin-Adair, 1958).

dropped) to establish private foundations along the lines of the establishment's multi-billion dollar giants.

So, whose fault was it that the voters were willing to grant to the Federal government the government's primary instrument of oppression in the United States, the Internal Revenue Service? Who was seducing whom? As I see it, there was larceny in everyone's heart in 1913. The difference between the conspirators and the victims was the difference between the professional con artist and the petty thief. I keep thinking of the movie, "The Sting." If the intended victim of a sting operation had not been a thief in his heart, and willing to cheat the professional con, the operation could not have worked. Or as the character Mordecai Jones (George C. Scott) says in "The Flim-Flam Man": "You can't cheat an honest man." What he was really saying was that virtually everyone he encountered was dishonest. The whole world was his potential victim.

A Moral Campaign

My contention is that my proposed educational campaign must be a lot more than just intellectual. It will involve a lot more than persuading the average voter of the existence of a conspiracy which is misusing political power to the detriment of most voters. What is needed is a *moral* campaign. Facts without a principle of interpretation are useless. Exposing a conspiracy without offering an alternative is wasted time. You can't beat something with nothing.

We need to appeal to free market principles, for they are *moral* principles. They are outworkings of explicitly biblical laws. I realize that some conservatives and most free market economists have not argued this way in the past, especially academic types. Professional academics (especially the economists) want to leave morality out of the discussion. They want "value-free" solutions. This invocation of "value-free" economics has failed, again and again. Society has conducted a continuing empirical test of this intellectual appeal, and has registered a verdict: *failure*. Besides, does anyone except economists really believe that there is moral neutrality in economics, psychology, political science, or anything else? Naive "value-free" faith has been under attack for two centuries, and fewer and fewer scholars have taken it seriously since 1965.[9]

The other side appeals to our basest instincts in order to manipulate us. But they are careful always to adopt the language of morality. They take what appears to be the moral high ground. They come before the voters "in the name of the People." They ask only to be allowed to serve the People. They want to act in the interests of the People. They want to "harness the engine of government" for the benefit of the People.

For eight or nine decades, this classic flim-flam has worked. Why? Because there is larceny in the hearts of the voters, and widespread ignorance of biblical morality ("thou shalt not steal, even by majority vote"), economics ("there ain't no such thing as a free lunch"), and the U.S. Constitution ("the delegation and dispersal of political power"). The proper response is to appeal to men's highest instincts, and to show them that the limited government philosophy and the free market economy are grounded in moral values that are among the highest that any civilization has ever adopted. We must take the moral high ground. Nothing else stands a chance of overturning the present power-drunk political system. We must appeal to *ethics* in order to overcome our opponents' raw power.

We must also understand that they, too, have a moral vision, a theology. Without it, they could never have been successful over the long haul. Ideas have consequences, for good or evil. We must understand our opponents' theology, and then do whatever we can to cleanse our own thinking of our opponents' first principles. If we adopt their first principles, then any fu-

---

9. The most important book which undermined the academic world's self-confidence in its own neutrality was Thomas Kuhn's *Structure of Scientific Revolutions* (2nd ed.; University of Chicago Press, 1970), first published in 1962.

ture competition between us and them is just another gangland struggle. Given the extent of their existing power, they will beat us every time.

3

THE CONSPIRACY'S THEOLOGY

Ye shall be as gods (Genesis 3:5).

What is the heart of the conspiracy's successful appeal, both to its members and to its eventual victims? Not the goodies that it promises, "comes the revolution." There are lots of ways of getting goodies in life. The real appeal is the appeal of a *uniquely revolutionary idea.* It is the same idea that the serpent presented to Eve: "Ye shall be as gods" (Genesis 3:5).

Men live by ideas, and no idea in man's history produced more evil than this one. Man, the god. Man, the predestinator. Man, the central planner. Man, the director of the evolutionary process. Man, the maker and shaker of things on earth and in the heavens. As Karl Marx's collaborator and financier Frederick Engels put it over a century ago, "man no longer merely proposes, but also disposes."[1] The chief premise of the modern conspirator is this: *Man, the savior of Man.*

This vision is inescapably religious. The impulse lying behind it is religious. Some have called it the religion of secular humanism. Others have called it the will to power (Nietzsche).

---

1. Frederick Engels, *Herr Eugen Dühring's Revolution in Science* [*Anti-Dühring*] (London: Lawrence & Wishart, [1877–78] 1934), p. 348.

But no one has described its implications better than C. S. Lewis:

> What we call man's power is, in reality, a power possessed by some men which they may, or may not, allow other men to profit by. . . . From this point of view, what we call Man's power over Nature turns out to be a power exercised by some men over other men with Nature as its instrument. . . . Man's conquest of Nature, if the dreams of some scientific planners are realized, means the rule of a few hundreds of men over billions upon billions of men. Each new power won *by* man is a power *over* man as well. Each advance leaves him weaker as well as stronger. In every victory, besides being the general who triumphs, he is also the prisoner who follows the triumphal car. . . . For the power of Man to make himself what he pleases means, as we have seen, the power of some men to make other men what *they* please.[2]

But there is something missing in Lewis' analysis. Must all progress necessarily lead to elitist power over others? If so, then we have a problem. If we proclaim the moral legitimacy of progress, and therefore the legitimacy of increasing man's power over his environment (power such as we possess with modern medicine), how are we to restrain the rise of power-drunk elites? Must we too become tyrants, just because we believe in historical progress?

Progress, after all, is not the product of cultural impotence. It involves the use of power. To avoid becoming tyrants, must we give up the idea of progress (as many in this century have done), and call for a retreat into mysticism? Are we to abandon the struggle against moral and social evil, in order to sit peacefully and contemplate our navels (or wait for the Rapture)? Are we culturally beaten before we start? In short, can we maintain

Biblical Progress/

---

2. C. S. Lewis, *The Abolition of Man* (New York: Macmillan, [1947] 1967), pp. 68, 69, 70, 71.

our own *vision of victory*—and every successful group in history always has possessed such a vision—and still prevent it from becoming just another stepping stone in the advance of political tyranny?

The answer is "yes, we can." But to achieve progress without tyranny, we must elevate *ethics* over power. This is what is missing from Lewis' summary (or at least missing from my summary of Lewis). We must recognize that in a cosmically personal universe, there are perpetually binding moral rules. These rules are ethical. They should remind us that all *autonomous* (self-made) power corrupts, and absolute autonomous power (in the hands of sinful creatures, meaning all of us) corrupts absolutely.

This does not mean that all power is evil. It is always necessary for righteous men to possess power if they are to reconstruct a civilization that has been run by evil men who possess raw power. The issue is ethics, not power as such. It depends on which ethical system a society adopts. Some ethical systems are evil. Marxism is a case in point. The question is: *Which ethical system?* One which elevates man and man's goals, or one which elevates God and therefore limits man's power? In short, do we proclaim the religion of God or the religion of humanism?

Limited Power

Western Civilization adopted biblical ethics as its moral foundation. The Bible teaches the sovereignty of God, not the sovereignty of man. What this means is that all creaturely power is inescapably *limited*. Man is a creature; he cannot possess ultimate power, and it is a sign of men's evil intentions if they pursue power as such—power divorced from ethics. All political power should therefore be limited by statute law and also by tradition, because man is a sinful creature. It means, in short, that man is not God. Power is delegated to specific men by God through other men, and all legitimate *delegated* power is therefore *limited* power.

The Old Testament required that the people of Israel be assembled once every seven years to hear the reading of God's law. Everyone was required to come: residents, children, women, priests, and rulers (Deuteronomy 31:9–13). No one was exempt. All were presumed to be able to understand the law. Everyone would know when the provisions of God's law were being violated. Thus, men had reasonable expectations about law enforcement. They could predict both the State and each other's actions far better, for all of them knew the *public, revealed law*.

Absolute authority ruled from the top: God. Limited authority was delegated from God to rulers, but only by means of revealed and fixed law.[3] The rulers could not legitimately change the law, and a bottom-up system of monitoring the rulers was established by the public reading of the law.

The U.S. Constitution, as a written document which binds the State itself, is an indirect product of this biblical approach. So is the common law jury system. A dozen of our peers are presumed to be better than robed judges at deciding both the facts and the law of the case. In any given judicial dispute, the decision of the jury is final. There is no double jeopardy: once declared innocent, the person cannot be retried for the same crime. The jury system is the last major bulwark against judicial tyranny.

Authority vs. Power

We need to understand that there is such a thing as *authority*. We must distinguish authority from power. Authority is limited power under God. It is *legitimate* power because it is *limited* by law and ethics. Political power must be limited if it is to remain

---

3. Gary North, *Leviticus: An Economic Commentary* (Tyler, Texas: Institute for Christian Economics, 1994), ch. 4.

legitimate. The Constitution's framers recognized this, and they attempted to construct a legal order which restrains political power. But to maintain itself from power-seekers of a rival faith, a society must be self-governed and self-restrained. Men must say to themselves, "My power is limited; therefore, the State's power is limited. The State is not Savior; therefore, the State is not absolutely sovereign. No appeal to the idea of the State as finally sovereign can be morally valid, and I will resist all such claims, and also those who make them."

Historically, this has meant that members of society must see themselves as under an authority other than the State. There has to be an enforcer somewhere. In the West, this has always meant God. For example, we added these words in the 1950's to our pledge of allegiance to the flag: "one nation, under God." Why? Because these words are consistent with American history. (Also, because Congress and the Supreme Court were not yet getting their concept of law from that ultimate "little old lady in tennis shoes," Madalyn Murray O'Hair.)[4] From the beginning, the essence of "the American experiment" was the attempt of wise men to design political institutions of legally limited power.

The limitation of civil power: this is what the U.S. Constitution was originally all about. This was what *The Federalist* was all about. While Hamilton was far more of a centralist than Madison, his political influence after 1800 collapsed dramatically. His view of the national government as the source of both political and economic unity did not take deep root in the United States until after the Civil War. Hamilton did not present a case for the expansive State in his essays in *The Federalist*. He wisely recognized that voters would be hostile to any such suggestion. Americans in 1787 did not trust the State, and they were wary

---

4. Mrs. O'Hair and several of her associates disappeared in early 1996. Her son Bill has been an evangelical Christian for over a decade.

of the proposed national government. They wanted it tied down with chains, which is why they insisted on a Bill of Rights.

It has been the essence of conspiracies throughout history to substitute power for ethics, and to substitute unrestricted power for limited authority. If one word summarizes the conspiratorial program, it is this one: *centralization*. In all things, the State is to be the pre-eminent power, the initiating agency as well as the final court of appeal.

There is no doubt that the two most representative revolutions in Western history were the American Revolution (and Constitutional settlement of 1789) and the French Revolution of 1789–94 (and the Napoleonic settlement of 1799–1815). Here we find the great political alternatives: the American decentralization of political power vs. the French centralization of political power; checks and balances vs. bureaucratic sovereignty; the jury system vs. administrative law; common law ("innocent until proven guilty") vs. Napoleonic law ("guilty until proven innocent"); common law precedents vs. Napoleonic codified law. In short, *bottom-up* society vs. *top-down* society. The Russian Revolution was simply a better-executed, more thoroughly centralized extension of the French Revolution.

The Church-State Alliance

There must be a sustaining philosophy—indeed, a sustaining religion—to undergird every society. Marx was incorrect: it is not the economic mode of production that undergirds the prevailing religious and philosophical ideals. Rather, *the ideals determine which sort of economy and political order can emerge*. We must not become "closet Marxists." We must not become economic determinists, Freudian determinists, or environmental determinists. Ethics is primary, not economics or political power.

There is always a necessary alliance between Church and State. This alliance need not be tyrannical. The two institutions need to be kept separate. But the alliance always exists. Without a broadly based sense of *moral legitimacy* concerning the civil government (or any institution which possesses power), rulers cannot rule their subjects indefinitely. To remove the king's throne, you must first remove the priests, or else convert their leaders to new beliefs. Anything less isn't a revolution; it is only a coup d'etat.

This shift in the thinking of influential priests literally took place in the decades before the French Revolution. That was one of the most brilliant and successful aspects of the program adopted by the conspirators who directed the French Revolution. A similar program was begun a century ago in the United States: the capture of seminaries, church boards,[5] and Christian colleges.[6] The National Council of Churches has been instrumental in this "capture of the robes."[7] Again and again, the money to fund this transformation after 1920 was provided by John D. Rockefeller, Jr., or one of the numerous Rockefeller foundations.[8]

To undermine a society, its opponents must first undermine men's faith in the existing moral and philosophical foundations of that society. This is why we find that in all cases of civilizations that have fallen into some version of the heresy of centralization, there has emerged a new alliance between Church and State, between new priests and kings, between new intelligentsia and politicians.

We must recognize that, in every era, anti-conspiratorialists also have their priests, kings, intelligentsia, and politicians. For every Jean Jacques Rousseau there is always an Edmund Burke.

---

5. Gary North, *Crossed Fingers: How the Liberals Captured the Presbyterian Church* (Tyler, Texas: Institute for Christian Economics, 1996).

6. George M. Marsden, *The Soul of the American University: From Protestant Establishment to Established Nonbelief* (New York: Oxford University Press, 1994).

7. C. Gregg Singer, *The Unholy Alliance* (New Rochelle, New York: Arlington House, 1975).

8. Albert F. Schenkel, *The Rich Man and the Kingdom: John D. Rockefeller, Jr., and the Protestant Establishment* (Minneapolis, Minnesota: Fortress, 1995).

For every Maximilien Robespierre there is always a George Washington. For every Karl Marx there is always a Eugen von Böhm-Bawerk. For every Karl Barth there is a Cornelius Van Til. For every Walter Lippmann there is always a Malcolm Muggridge. In short, for every Arius there is always an Athanasius. The question is never "kings, priests, politicians, and intelligentsia *vs.* no kings, priests, politicians, and intelligentsia." It is always a question of *"whose?"*

Fractional Reserve Banking

Now try this one: for every David Rockefeller there is always a . . . ?

All of a sudden, it gets more difficult to identify a good guy on the other side. In this one realm, banking, there seems to be no good guy lurking in the historical wings. There may be nice merchant bankers and central bankers. Somewhere. Perhaps. There are no doubt rulers of great banking empires who love their children and donate money to the Society for the Prevention of Cruelty to Animals. But what we seem to be short of is presidents of major commercial banks or directors of central banks who cry out against the use of fractional reserve banking to centralize power at the expense of the public in general and borrowers in particular. Why is this?

Because modern banking is fractional reserve banking, it inescapably involves fraud. It also creates the boom-bust business cycle—a cycle which the manipulators can use to their advantage because they control the mechanism by which it is created: the money supply.[9]

This is not the place to go into the details of the process by which fractional reserve banking produces counterfeit money, and why governments exempt the banking system from prosecution against counterfeiting. Murray Rothbard has described

---

9. Ludwig von Mises, *Human Action: A Treatise on Economics* (3rd ed.; Chicago: Regnery, 1966), ch. 20.

the process more clearly than anyone ever has in his classic little booklet, _What Has Government Done to Our Money?_, which you can (and should) buy from the Mises Institute, Auburn, Alabama. I've never read anything better on money. Let me simply say that the monopoly of fractional reserve banking is inherently corrupt, inherently a process of legalized theft, and inherently power-seeking.

When you deposit, say, a check for $100 into your bank, the bank takes about $10 of that money and sends it to the Federal Reserve System, our nation's partially private and partially governmental central bank. The FED pays no interest on the money. This $10 serves as a legal reserve for the money. Now, your banker makes money by lending money. He takes the $90 and loans it out. The fellow who borrows it then spends it. The recipient takes the $90 and deposits it in _his_ bank. His banker takes $9 and sends it to the FED. Then he loans $81 to some borrower, who spends it, and the recipient takes the $81 to his bank.

You get the picture. In theory, $900 can come into circulation on the basis of your original deposit of $100, if the reserve ratio is set at 10%. This is the "genius" of fractional reserve banking. If you wonder why we have inflation in the modern world, here is a good place to begin looking.

Who, then, controls the Federal Reserve System? And why was it established? Why was it, in the words of Thibaut de Saint Phalle, _an intentional mystery_?[10]

Again and again, the story of Establishment conspiracy returns to the big New York banking firms. For centuries, the plans of the conspirators have originated in conference rooms of the great banks, or in conjunction with the banking establishment.[11] Why? Because money is the central institution in a

---

10. Thibaut de Saint Phalle, _The Federal Reserve System: An Intentional Mystery_ (New York: Praeger, 1985).

11. John Brewer, _The Sinews of Power: War, Money and the English State, 1688–1783_ (New York: Knopf, 1988); P. G. M. Dickson, _The Financial Revolution in England:_

division-of-labor economy; therefore, control over the issue of money becomes the single-most-important grant of monopoly privilege that the national government can make to any private or quasi-public organization. Those who receive such a monopolistic grant know how to use it to their advantage. Those who do not receive it seldom understand the process of money creation, the benefits it gives to those who do understand, and the catastrophes such monopolistic power invariably has led to in history.

This ignorance benefits the money creators. Monetary theory is so little understood by the public (including legislators and judges), and monetary institutions are so mysterious—they were designed to be that way, especially central banks—that once established, only catastrophic economic events, or a dedicated leader (such as President Andrew Jackson), can ever produce a meaningful reform. The supposed reforms otherwise go from bad to worse, from less centralized to more centralized.

The Unification of Man

We are monotheists in the West. The god of our civilization must be a unified god. For over a thousand years, the West, being Christian (with local Jewish subdivisions), historically affirmed the unity of mankind. All men are created in the image of God, who is Himself unified. But, at the same time, orthodox Christians and orthodox (uncapitalized) Jews—I don't limit this to Orthodox Jews alone—have always simultaneously proclaimed that mankind is *divided ethically.* There are good men and bad men, saved and lost, saints and sinners, covenant-keepers and covenant-breakers. Thus, the goal of the unification of mankind is necessarily limited. Men will never be unified ethically. There will always be a struggle between good and evil. The conspiracy will always be around. The point is, then, to construct *institutions that will preserve the peace*—civil, ecclesias-

---

A Study in the Development of Public Credit, 1688–1756 (London: Macmillan, 1967).

tical, educational, economic, etc.—but which will also suppress the *outward manifestations* of evil. Warning: outward, *not* inward evil.

In the West, we have always recognized that God saves men, not the State. Laws must suppress outward evil, but they must never be designed to *save* men ethically. The State is not God. It is not supposed to make men good; it is only supposed to restrain men from public evil acts. The State has not been granted the power to replace God as Savior. Thus, Western Civilization has historically avoided the doctrine of *salvation by law*, especially statist law. Whenever and wherever the doctrine of salvation by civil law has been preached, then and there we have found a conspiracy against Western Civilization.

The motivation of conspiracies is simple: to be as God. The conspiracies of the West, being Western, have also adopted the notion of *the unity of the godhead*. But who is this god? It is *man himself*. To achieve (evolve to) this position of divinity, men therefore need to be unified—not just unified through voluntary co-operation (such as in a free market transaction), but *unified ethically*.

It would be futile to attempt to list all the statements by humanist scholars that proclaim the need for the unification of man. A representative example is an interview with Carl Sagan, the popular astronomer (I am tempted to write "pop astronomer") whose multimillion dollar 1980 Public Broadcasting System show, "Cosmos," was a 12-week propaganda blast for evolution. Sagan writes:

> I'd say that our strengths are a kind of intelligence and adaptability. In the last few thousand years, we've made astonishing cultural and technical advances. In other areas, we've not made so much progress. For example, we are still bound up in sectarian and national rivalries.

"Intelligence and adaptability" are code words for evolution, meaning man-directed *social, political, and economic* evolution. "Sectarian and national rivalries" are code words for religious differences and nationalism. But Sagan is optimistic. He sees a new world a-comin'. Some people might even call it the New World Order.

> It's clear that sometime relatively soon in terms of the lifetime of the human species people will identify with the entire planet and the species, provided we don't destroy ourselves first. That's the race I see us engaged in—a contest between unifying the planet and destroying ourselves."[12]

Back in the 1950's, the slogan was: "Peace in the world, or the world in pieces." It is the same religious pitch: the unification of mankind ethically and politically—the one-world order—is necessary if mankind is to survive as a species. Men must have the very similar moral, political, and economic goals. Divisive creeds and opinions need to be educated out of people, preferably by means of compulsory, tax-financed schools. Diversity of opinion concerning these "humanistic" goals must not be tolerated, meaning "sectarian and national rivalries." Mankind must not be allowed to reveal differences of opinion on fundamentals. Mankind's godhead is at stake.

Now, there are three ways to achieve this unity: persuasion ("conversion"), manipulation, and execution. The first approach takes forever, or at least it seems to take forever. It also eats up lots of resources. It takes teams of "missionaries." People just never seem to agree on these humanistic first principles. They bicker. They battle. They refuse to be persuaded. Mankind reveals its lack of agreement on religion and ethics. This, you understand, must not be tolerated.

---

12. *U.S. News and World Report* (Oct. 21, 1985), p. 66.

If you cannot persuade men to co-operate, either by force of reason, or an appeal to self-interest, or moral appeal, then you have only two choices remaining: manipulation or execution. Either you confuse the bickering factions by means of an endless process of shifting alliances, thereby gaining their co-operation under a unified (but necessarily secret) elite of planners, or else one faction must eliminate all rivals by force: you kill your opponents, or make them slaves. There is no third alternative, given the false doctrine of the ethical unity of man. Man is in principle ethically unified, this theology proclaims; therefore, any visible deviations from this hypothetical unity must be suppressed, one way or another.

This brings us to the next phase of conspiracy analysis. We need to ask ourselves: Which kind of conspiracy?

4

TWO KINDS OF CONSPIRACY

And it came to pass, when Rehoboam had established the kingdom, and had strengthened himself, he forsook the law of the Lord, and all Israel with him. And it came to pass, that in the fifth year of king Rehoboam Shishak king of Egypt came up against Jerusalem, because they had transgressed against the Lord (II Chronicles 12:1–2).

Rehoboam is not a familiar name in Bible history. He was Solomon's son, and he inherited the kingdom of Israel at its high point: more wealth, influence, and power than it was ever to experience again.

Early in his reign, the people came before him and asked that he reduce their taxes. For three days he consulted with his counsellors. The older counsellors agreed with the people, but not the younger ones. Rehoboam sided with the younger ones. He came before the representatives of the tribes and promised to hike taxes. "My father hath chastised you with whips, but I will chastise you with scorpions" (I Kings 12:12). Within weeks, the rebel leader Jeroboam led ten tribes out of the old kingdom and established a new nation, Israel (the northern kingdom), leaving Rehoboam to strut over and threaten only two tribes, Judah and Benjamin (the southern kingdom). Rehoboam's conspiracy against the people caused a civil war and had split the kingdom permanently.

Rehoboam learned slowly. First he had conspired against the people of Israel. Next, he rebelled against God. He took his much-reduced kingdom into ethical war against God—the old error of conspirators throughout history, both human and angelic. Then Shishak of Egypt prepared to invade. The original slave-holding tyranny threatened again. This time, Rehoboam repented, along with the princes (II Chronicles 12:6). God then repented in part, but He brought Shishak in for a raid. God gave them "some deliverance" (II Chronicles 12:7).

This was Israel's recurring lesson, which the people never really learned. Conspire against the law of God, and you thereby conspire against God. God then brings in full judgment: invasion. Again and again, He did this with Israel. When the kings conspired against God, they found themselves at the mercy of the really ruthless conspirators, the rival pagan empires. The rivals always possessed greater power than the half-hearted conspirators of Israel. The rulers of Israel dabbled in the occult, dabbled in the power religion, dabbled in rebellion against God, and dabbled in tyranny. They were no match for the full-time conspirators, once God let them go.

Unification: Two Strategies

The average citizen knows about various conspiracies that proclaim "unification through execution." We have seen their work in history: the Jacobins in the French Revolution, the Bolshevik Party in the Russian Revolution, and Aryan masters of the Nazi revolution. They achieve "consensus by terror"—endless terror, Karl Marx's vision of "the revolution in permanence."[1] The old description is true: "The Revolution

---

1. Karl Marx, "Address of the Central Committee to the Communist League" (1850), in Karl Marx and Frederick Engels, *Selected Works*, 3 vols. (Moscow: Progress Publishers, 1969), I, p. 185.

eats its children." (I like the wit's addition: "But not soon enough.")

What the average citizen does not readily recognize is the existence of the other form of conspiratorial organization, the kind described in *None Dare Call It Conspiracy*. This kind bases its strategy and tactics on the principle of "unification through manipulation." This form of conspiracy operates under a very different set of presuppositions and assumptions about the way to achieve universal ethical unity. Its pre-eminent hypothesis is this: *ideology is ultimately irrelevant.* Ideological differences cannot possibly be ultimate, for we know that all ultimate disagreements are ethical disagreements, and mankind cannot possibly be ethically divided. By definition, any perceived ethical disunity just has to be a temporary phenomenon. To admit that such ethical disunity is fundamental and permanent is to admit that mankind is not God, for God cannot be ethically divided against Himself. Therefore, they reject the idea. They believe that there are always ways to overcome ethical (ideological) disunity. = unification thru execution.

The best way to overcome this temporary disunity, of course, is to make a deal, preferably a business deal. Best of all, make a business deal at taxpayers' expense.

Conspiratorial humanists all agree that mankind *ought* to be unified ethically, where all men share the same cosmic vision. But they disagree about the hypothesis that mankind *is*, in fact, ethically unified. The "conspirators through execution" acknowledge that all men clearly are not yet ethically unified; therefore, some men—indeed, millions of them—will have to be removed from visible existence (execution, the Gulag) if they persist in their rebellion against the Truth. What kind of Truth? Jacobin Truth, proletarian Truth, or Nazi Truth: they all argue (and act) the same way. The pattern is repeated because the theology is repeated.

In contrast, the "conspirators through manipulation" dare not admit such a thing. To do so would deny their theological

or vice versa

premise of the *existing* underlying ethical unity of mankind, meaning "mankind properly understood." They, of course, are just the people to "properly understand" mankind, whether mankind agrees with them or not.

Secrecy

What these manipulating conspirators need is *secrecy*. They realize that at this stage of history, men publicly disagree about the fundamentals. If they try to "hold mankind together" by serving as intermediaries between (or among) various warring societies, they need to do so invisibly. Voters in the United States never wanted to join together in a one-world government with the Soviet Union. They knew full well who would have been the policeman in such a society. If "conspirators through manipulation" had tried to persuade the average American voter to allow them to move forward in the creation of such a New World Order of ethically unified humanity, they would not have gained co-operation. The collapse of the Soviet Union in 1991 has now made this project irrelevant. The question now is: How soon will former Communist states be brought into NATO and the other internationalist organizations?

The conspirators always kept their program of long-term convergence relatively quiet. I say "relatively." Since 1973, the Trilateral Commission has published its intention repeatedly to create a New World Order. Doesn't this refute my contention that they are a conspiracy? Aren't all conspiracies always completely secret?

No, they aren't. Adam Weishaupt's Illuminati were almost entirely secret. But, as time goes on, the conspirators have become more open, especially the "conspirators by execution." Hitler published *Mein Kampf*. Lenin published his intentions repeatedly. True, they did not announce their intention to liquidate specific numbers of specific groups, but they announced their general intentions. But hardly anyone in power believed them. Why not? Because the "conspirators by manipulation" always said that these were just verbal excesses. "They really don't mean it! So let's make a deal."

But aren't all "conspiracies through manipulation" always secret all the time? No, they aren't. They are secret about *some* things. They were secret about the real intentions of the Federal Reserve System before it was voted into law in 1913. They were secret about the real intentions of the Federal income tax before it was voted into law (or more accurately, before voters were *told* that it had been voted into law) in 1913. But some of their program has always public. Their "helpful guys" image is carefully maintained. Nevertheless, prior to Dan Smoot's *Invisible Government* (1962), the C.F.R. kept an incredibly low profile.

Books and Covers

Books, however, were always a high priority item. The C.F.R. is always bringing out books. So are its members. Bland, boring books. One important C.F.R. outlet is Praeger Publishers. How many variations of titles and books have appeared that are along the lines of Richard N. Gardner's (Harvard U., Harvard Law School, Rhodes scholar, Oxford Ph.D., Deputy Assistant Secretary of State, and, of course, C.F.R.) *In Pursuit of World Order: U.S. Foreign Policy and International Organizations* (Praeger, 1965), with a foreword by Harlan Cleveland (C.F.R.)? Hundreds? Thousands? Who cares? Too many, at the very least. (For more on Gardner, see my Preface, page xiii.)

Here is this book, written by a man with impeccable academic credentials, who writes a book with a very "peccable" thesis: that the United Nations is an institution which offers the world hope. I happen to have bought a used copy, probably for under a dollar, at some long-forgotten used book sale. It is an autographed copy. It is dedicated to someone as follows: "With gratitude for his contributions to the pursuit of world order through 'UN We Believe,' Best Wishes, Richard N. Gardner." Maybe it's a forgery. Anyway, forgery or not, it still sold for under a dollar.

How could this earnest-looking man in his late thirties have devoted himself to such a preposterous task, to prove that the UN offers anyone hope in anything except, possibly, a bureaucratic job in some UN agency? How could Adlai E. Stevenson, Hubert H. Humphrey, Henry Cabot Lodge, and Sen. Jacob K. Javits have all written blurbs for it on the back of the dust jacket? There is only one reasonable conclusion: none of them actually read this pathetic little book, with its dry, brief descriptions of endless UN agencies (GATT, UNCSAT, ICAO, WHO, FAO, etc., etc.), and its hopeful chapter titles, such as "Turning Point in World Trade" and "Solving the Monetary Dilemma." It took a Rhodes scholar to write this?

Books make them look scholarly. Books make them look respectable. Books make them look like a bunch of academics, meaning powerless. Adam Weishaupt, founder of the Illuminati, an important late-eighteenth-century secret revolutionary society,[2] recognized the importance of books very early. He laid down guidelines concerning the proper concealment of a secret society. No principle was more important than looking unimportant. Books were part of this cover.

> The great strength of our Order lies in its concealment; let it never appear in any place in its own name, but always covered by another name, and another occupation. *None is fitter than the three lower degrees of Free Masonry; the public is accustomed to it, expects little from it, and therefore takes little notice of it.* Next to this, the form of a learned or literary society is best suited to our purpose, and had Free Masonry not existed, this cover would have been employed; and it may be much more than a cover, *it may be a powerful engine in our hands. By establishing reading societies, and subscription libraries, and taking these under our direction, and supplying them through our labours, we may turn the public mind which way we will. . . .* A Literary Society is the most proper form for

---

2. James Billington, *Fire in the Minds of Men: Origins of the Revolutionary Faith* (New York: Basic Books, 1980), pp. 93–99.

the introduction of our Order into any state where we are yet strangers.[3]

Today, the college and university have taken the place of reading societies. So have literary reviews and book review services, so that lazy pseudo-intellectuals can appear to be well-informed without actually having to read fat books. Discussion groups have replaced the literary society. And the biggest discussion group of all is the Council on Foreign Relations.

But that was only the beginning, Weishaupt said. "In like manner we must try to obtain an influence in the military academies (this may be of mighty consequence), the printing-houses, booksellers shops, chapters, and in short all offices which have any effect, either in forming, or in managing, or even in directing the mind of man: painting and engraving are highly worth our care."[4]

Weishaupt's strategy still holds. First, the military academies and the military. The Commandant of West Point over the last generation has always been a C.F.R. member.[5] Senior commanders are also CFR members. The C.F.R. sponsored many meetings around the country in 1983–84, as it does every year—meetings that featured C.F.R. members in the military. These members included: Bernard W. Rogers, Supreme Allied Commander, Europe; John W. Vessey, Jr., Chairman, Joint Chiefs of Staff; John A. Wickham, Jr., Chief of Staff, U.S. Army; John T. Chain, Deputy Chief of Staff, Plans and Operations, U.S. Air Force; Paul F. Gorman, Commander-in-Chief, United States Southern Command, etc.[6] The most spectacular case is that of Gen. Al Haig, a mediocre West Point student, who was

---

3. Quoted in John Robison, *Proofs of a Conspiracy* (1798); reprinted by Western Islands, Boston, 1967, p. 112.

4. *Ibid.*

5. Susan Huck, "Lost Valor," *American Opinion* (October 1977); "Military," *American Opinion* (July/August 1980).

6. Council on Foreign Relations, *Annual Report 1983–1984*, p. 56.

a colonel when he joined Henry Kissinger's staff in 1969. Four years later, he was a four-star general, skipping the third star (lieutenant general) completely. He catapulted over 240 other general officers.[7] He later served as Secretary of State under President Reagan. Not bad for a "verbally challenged" guy!

Second, publishing. Every secret agent needs a "cover." Every conspiracy also needs a cover, as Weishaupt said. Academic books have for two centuries been part of the manipulators' cover. But remember North's law of "harmless" conspiracies: *you shouldn't judge a cover by its books*. The books may be bland and boring, but their authors are not harmless.

The Trilateral Commission

Things have changed since 1970 that have forced the manipulators to become more open about *part* of their activities. Millions of Americans now know who they are and what they are. It is now impossible for them to hide completely. So they are attempting to deflect the charge of "conspiracy" by going partially public. This tactic can be seen in David Rockefeller's defense of the Trilateral Commission in a letter to the editor in the *New York Times* (August 25, 1980):

> Is the commission secretive? Not at all. For $10 a year, anyone can subscribe to its quarterly magazine, "Trialogue," and also receive periodic mailings of task force reports. Furthermore, we publish a list of the source of all U.S. contributions in excess of $5,000. The only part of our proceedings that is "off the record" are discussions at commission meetings, and we keep these private to encourage uninhibited criticism and debate.

His letter was clearly pulled out of a computerized word processor, for this canned response contains whole paragraphs

---

7. Gary Allen, *Kissinger: The Secret Side of the Secretary of State* (Seal Beach, California: '76 Press, 1976), p. 119.

that were reprinted in the *Saturday Evening Post* (October 1980) two months later: "The Trilateral Commission Explained," by David Rockefeller.

A subscription to a magazine which carries no advertising, plus "periodic mailings of task force reports," all for $10 a year! Not a profit-seeking magazine, surely. No, a subsidized propaganda magazine from a secret society that had to be created in 1973 in order to help deflect the heat after 1972 that books like *None Dare Call It Conspiracy* had produced for the C.F.R. The Trilateral Commission is a kind of heat shield. It is public where it has to be, secret where it has to be ("discussion group secrecy"), and conspiratorial from day one.

"Conspiracy," Plus What Else?

The conspirators hope that people will not believe the story that is contained in a book such as *None Dare Call It Conspiracy*. Secrecy has been basic to their plans. This secrecy is not so secure as it was prior to 1960. But they still use the tactic of ridiculing all conspiracy theories of history, as we have seen. So they have adopted the tactic of ridiculing as infantile everyone who advocates a conspiracy view of history.

Contrary to what you might think, conspiracy theories can be very sophisticated. They do not simply rely on exposing any particular group of conspirators and then proclaiming, "These people did it to us!" On the contrary, a serious conspiracy theorist relies heavily on social and economic analysis, especially the analysis of ideas: the "climate of opinion."

Let me demonstrate what I mean. The American public's opinion is changing. People are starting to reject the political ideas that allowed the creation of the conspiratorial system of economic control. Will the public now be able to dislodge the power-brokers? If they believe in the existence of this conspiracy, won't the public reaction against domestic socialism accelerate? The opposition thinks so.

The climate of opinion in America is shifting. Ask yourself: "What is more important, the shift in the climate of opinion, or the new facts that bring the book up to date?" If you agree with me about the importance of widely shared ideas, you will say, "the shift in the climate of opinion is more important than the new edition." In other words, it is the *big picture* that dominates—the shift in opinion of millions of Americans, *as well as a growing minority of articulate intellectuals*—rather than the effects of some paperback books of the early 1970's. (Unless you want to argue that the earlier books were the primary cause of the shift in the climate of opinion—and I don't think any of the authors is arrogant enough to say it, or stupid enough to think it.)

The Climate of Opinion

Let me put it another way. If some conspirator had put a Mafia contract on Gary Allen, Larry Abraham, and W. Cleon Skousen in 1968, and they had all been murdered, and if *None Dare* and *Naked Capitalist* had never been published, would the shift of opinion still be going on? Almost certainly.

All right, let's take it one step farther. Do you think that if someone had put a bomb into a room filled with Rockefellers, Carnegies, and the other conspirators of 1913, no matter how early in the game, do you think their deaths would have stopped the erosion of Constitutional liberties? Yes? No? Maybe? I did not say *slowed* the erosion; I said *stopped*.

I'll bet you don't believe that a bomb would have stopped it. Shoot one enemy, and another one appears, *on either side of the conflict*. Why? Because it is the struggle—a *religious* struggle over the acceptable world-and-life view, the first principles of society—which is central, not the specific conspirators. It is the script, not the players, which is central.

Yes, there are important participants. John D. Rockefeller, Jr., was one. J. Pierpont Morgan was one. "Col." E. M. House was one. But if all three had died at age ten, would the fight over the right to interpret the U.S. Constitution not have taken place? Would it have been a "slam dunk" (to use a basketball analogy) for the good guys? Of course not.

So, what does this say about conspiracies? *Like weeds, they need a field to grow in.* The field is a climate of opinion—the same field used by the rulers of any society. Change the ideas, and you change the social order. The real conflict is not over money, or military hardware, or votes. *The real conflict is over ideas.*

One more question. How widespread does the *dominant* climate of opinion have to be in order for a ruling elite—and all rulers are part of an elite—to maintain control? Does almost everyone in a society need to share the basic presuppositions of the leaders, or only the literate minority which writes and speaks "in the name of" the people, or the Party, or the *Volk*, or the evolutionary forces of history, or God Himself? In other words, if a conspiracy gains control of the *prestigious outlets for ideas*, can its members continue to control the lives of the masses? If not, why not?

We might put it this way: If a conspiracy persuades the vast majority of a society to change their opinions and agree with the conspirators, can we legitimately cry "foul"? Wouldn't public debate really eliminate the conspiratorial aspect of the articulate minority? If we answer, "yes, it was all done in the open according to the rules," then when we talk about a conspiracy, we must be talking about a group that *doesn't* do it by the rules. What, then, are the rules—the *good and righteous rules*—of political competition? And have today's leaders played by these rules? (Hint: when you think of rules of the game, think "Constitution." Furthermore, think "law of God, as revealed in the Bible.")

The conspiracy is powerful. But the key to stopping the conspiracy is above all *educational.* If it were simply a matter of personal power, a few bombs would do the job. Neither side believes in the power of bombs, as such. What distinguished Lenin from two generations of suicidal Russian revolutionaries was that Lenin believed in centralized Party discipline, newspaper articles, tracts, books, and bombs—probably in that order. Bombs were in last place, as the October Revolution proved in 1917. He captured Russia virtually without firing a shot. Why was he able to do this? Because the Russian rulers, like the Russian people, had lost faith in the moral and intellectual foundations of Old Russia.

Also, the Czar had a massive centralized bureaucracy, all ready and waiting to be captured.[8] So, for that matter, did Louis XVI of France in 1789.[9]

So it is not simply a question of conspiratorial mobilization. It is a question of conspiratorial mobilization *within a particular climate of opinion and within particular historical circumstances.* Conspirators understand this best of all. They also understand that if any hostile critic of their actions dares to mention the existence of their conspiracy, which has been successful in *using* the climate of opinion to manipulate the majority, he can be cut off at the knees simply by sneering, "Oh, yes, a conspiracy thesis of history. How infantile."

That sneer, coupled with threats to professional careers, has worked incredibly well. So, academic outsiders necessarily have to do the initial work, people such as Dan Smoot, who wrote the first major exposé of the Council on Foreign Relations, *The Invisible Government* (1962), got it published by a small conservative maverick publisher, and then sold an incredible one million copies through the mails because he had his own weekly T.V. show. The same is true of Allen, Abraham, and Skousen. These men understood Rushdoony's principle that "intellectual respectability in the eyes of either the liberals or anyone else is an irrelevant matter in the discussion of any question. We must leave the dead to bury the dead."[10]

---

8. Richard Pipes, *Russia Under the Old Regime* (New York: Scribner's, 1974).

9. Alexis de Tocqueville, *The Old Regime and The French Revolution* (4th ed.; Gloucester, Massachusetts: Peter Smith, [1858] 1987).

10. R. J. Rushdoony, *The Nature of the American System* (Fairfax, Virginia: Tho-

Dead and dying men, however, continue to be outraged. Nevertheless, they must keep their outrage concealed. They must appear to be calm, cool, and collected. So they have hired other men to do their work for them. Instead of an outraged cry against conservatives who resist international political convergence, they have hired historians, political scientists, and newspaper editorialists to do their sneering for them. It worked for many decades. It isn't working so well these days.

burn Press, [1965] 1978), p. 141.

5

COURT HISTORIANS

*For they prophesy a lie unto you, to remove you far from your land;
and that I should drive you out, and ye should perish (Jeremiah 27:10).*

In Israel, there were priests who taught the people and who
administered the sacrifices of the temple. When they periodical-
ly grew lax and fell into disbelief, God would raise up prophets
who came before the rulers and the people. These prophets
would remind them of what God had done for them, what God
had done to their enemies, and what God would surely do to
them in the future if they persisted in acting like their religious
enemies.

The rebellious kings did not appreciate the message of the
prophets. To counter this message, and to comfort the rulers,
the kings would surround themselves with false prophets.
These men would declare in the name of God all the good
news that the kings wanted to hear. Some kings may even have
begun to believe these court prophets, but not all of them did.

The worst of the bunch, King Ahab, plotted with King Jeho-
shephat of Judah against the king of Syria. Jehosephat wanted
Ahab to ask the prophets if God was going to give them a victory. All the 400 of the court prophets predicted victory. But
Jehoshaphat wanted "a second opinion." Wasn't another proph-

et available for consultation? Only Micaiah, said Ahab, "but I hate him; for he doth not phophesy good concerning me, but evil" (I Kings 22:8). But Ahab called him to the court anyway.

Micaiah gave the standard, "you're a winner, king" prophecy. It was fake, and both of them knew it. "And the king said unto him, How many times shall I adjure thee that thou tell me nothing but that which is true in the name of the Lord? (22:16). So Micaiah told him the truth: he would be killed. "And the king of Israel said unto Jehoshaphat, Did I not tell thee that he would prophesy no good concerning me, but evil?" (22:18). Ahab knew the difference between a true prophet of God and his 400 hired prophets. He went to battle anyway, and was slain.

Centuries later, Jeremiah confronted another band of hired prophets. They were singing the same old song: the evil king would be victorious. Not so, said Jeremiah: he would lead the nation of Judah into captivity to Babylon, just as Israel had already gone into captivity to Assyria a century earlier for their sins. But the king did not listen. They went into captivity. Instead of telling the king and the people to repent from their sins, the court prophets had proclaimed victory. The result was defeat.

Hired Historians

Kings in the ancient world not only hired court prophets to proclaim future tidings of great joy, they also hired literate record-keepers who would proclaim the wonders of kingly rule. They paid for a glorious past as well as a glorious future. The court historians served enthusiastically. Perhaps the most influential court historian in Western history was the former Jewish zealot and revolutionary, Josephus, who switched sides in the nick of time and became an official historian for the Roman emperors Vespasian and Titus, who conquered Jerusalem in 69–70 A.D.

This ancient if not particularly honorable profession is with us still. Governments have numerous historians employed in one capacity or another, and not just as archivists. Private agencies, especially tax-exempt foundations, also employ them. Their unstated purpose is to present in the best possible light—given the limits of public acceptance—past government policies. Their function is retroactively to validate the official explanations.

It is not surprising that the British government has a 30-year "incubation" period for the legal release of its diplomatic files, and that any official who writes memoirs that relate to "protected" documents must have the memoirs approved before publication, in order to guarantee that official secrets are not revealed. It is also not surprising that the Warren Commission sealed off a number of documents (photos) concerning the Kennedy assassination for 75 years, and that the 26-volume compilation of the evidence has no index. (One solution has been to put the entire set on a CD-ROM disk with electronic search software included.)

The Conspiracy View of History

The conspiracy view of history is based on the following presuppositions. First, people make history; impersonal forces do not. Second, events do take place within historical limits: economics, politics, ideas, etc. Third, powerful people are powerful. Fourth, powerful people seek to achieve their goals by means of public and quasi-public institutions that are financed by the general public, including their enemies. Fifth, in order to achieve many of these goals, the planners need to conceal their plans from their enemies. Events must be made to seem spontaneous and beyond the power of the leaders to control. Alternatively, events must be directed and made to appear as side-effects of other policies of which the public approves.

In short, the conspiracy view of history argues that self-interested people do get together to conspire against the interests of the public at large, or at least against the interests of the public *as the public would interpret the facts, if they really understood what was going on.* These acts need not be illegal in order to qualify as a conspiracy-view version of conspiracy. We are not necessarily speaking here of a violation of a nation's conspiracy statutes. Sometimes, however, we are talking about such a conspiracy. But a successful conspiracy probably cannot be prosecuted within the seven-year statute of limitations because the conspirators control the office of prosecutor.

The conspiracy view of history has been unpopular in our day. It is especially unpopular in university classrooms, though not so unpopular as it was in the classroom prior to 1965. Scholars prefer to talk more about impersonal historical forces, or the climate of opinion, or random events, or economic determinism, or just about anything except clandestine groups of self-interested manipulators, especially conspirators who have been *quietly* successful (as distinguished from Lenin and Hitler, who were visibly successful).

The Marxists are more willing to discuss specific manipulations by monopoly capitalists. New Left historians have written histories of America and England that lend themselves to conspiracy historians who do not share their Marxist presuppositions. Perhaps the best example is the use that conservative and libertarian historians have made of Gabriel Kolko's study of the Progressive movement, *The Triumph of Conservatism* (1963).[1] The book made little academic impact when it was first published, but then the Kennedy assassination and the revival of conspiracy theories rescued it. Kolko argues that the liberal, reformist rhetoric of the Progressive movement was in fact a cover for big businesses that used the power of the Federal

---

1. Gabriel Kolko, *The Triumph of Conservatism: A Reinterpretation of American History, 1900–1916* (New York: Free Press of Glencoe, 1963).

government to establish monopolies that became insulated from price competition from newer, more innovative firms. This is what the free market "Chicago School" economists have concluded, too, as have Murray Rothbard and his followers, who are in turn followers of free market economist Ludwig von Mises.

Yet even here, there is an exception: the Federal Reserve System. Free market economists who are ready to label all the Progressive era Federal regulatory agencies as self-interested, competition-reducing bureaucracies accept the Federal Reserve System—privately owned—as a public-spirited organization. Typical is the standard economics textbook by Gwartney and Stroup. Its perspective is that of the "public choice" school of economics, noted for its adherents' rigor in seeking out hidden, self-serving agendas of government bureaucrats and agencies. But not when it comes to central banking: "The major purpose of the Federal Reserve System (and other central banks) is to regulate the money supply and provide a monetary climate that is in the best interest of the entire economy."[2] So much for public choice economic theory.

Economic historians are not generally conspiracy theorists. They are ready to discuss personal self-interest of groups that seek power, but they usually shy away from any theory which asserts that economic interests are so uniform that a clandestine group of conspirators can use the State successfully to hold off competitive market forces for decades. They do not want to admit that the public can be hoodwinked that long. They want to see people as rational, and the interests of conspirators are not the same as the interests of voters. The voters will eventually catch on. A century of domination by an elitist group is just not conceivable for your typical economic historian. A decade, yes; two decades, maybe; but not a century. Only if the climate

2. James D. Gwartney and Richard L. Stroup, *Economics: Private and Public Choice* (4th ed.; New York: Harcourt Brace Jovanovich, 1982), p. 281.

of opinion matches up with economic self-interest could a conspiracy rule that long—and then only if the conspiracy really did represent the people's best interests. But then it would not be a conspiracy any longer.

Relativism

But wait a minute. Those of us who hold a conspiracy view of history are also interested in discussing the climate of opinion, or economic forces that create the historical setting for a shift in the climate of opinion. What is the difference between our interpretation and the interpretations of conventional classroom historians? The difference is this: the conspiratorialists know that there is a *continuing* ideological and theological war going on. Different players, same issues. New faces, same conflict. Those who favor a conspiracy view argue that there are fundamental issues—moral, religious, and political issues—that divide good from evil, good guys from bad guys. In short, conspiracy buffs usually are opposed to ethical relativism. They tend to be moral absolutists. They view history as a continuing personal struggle between the forces of good and the forces of evil.

This is what outrages professional historians, including most economic historians. (An exception was Murray Rothbard, who believes in natural law and permanent ethical standards, and who was ready to consider almost any conspiracy theory.) They are weaned on a diet of ethical relativism; this perspective is basic to all the social sciences and humanities. They will admit today that Stalin was evil (by *today's* standards). "But we need to understand that in his time, and confronting the situation of an economically backward nation, Stalin faced tremendous difficulties in modernizing Russia, so measures that we now regard as extreme had to be imposed . . . blah, blah, blah."

On the other hand, Hitler was absolutely evil. (Goodbye relativism—or so it initially appears.) Don't push them on why it is more evil to slaughter Jews than kulak peasants. They grow evasive. Why? Because their bottom line on political morality is pure pragmatism. The basis of their absolute opposition to Hitler boils down to this: Stalin, Churchill, and F.D.R. beat Hitler. In short, *Hitler was a loser*. He was a conspirator who got caught before he had consolidated his power. Herein lies his offense. To use language from another discipline, he went for an inside straight, and missed.

There was a period before the War when he looked as though he would be successful. In this period (you will never be told in any university classroom), some very powerful and influential Americans were sending him money. The same sorts of people who sent Lenin money. The same sorts of people who got Franklin Roosevelt elected. People on Wall Street. People who belong to, or have belonged to, the Council on Foreign Relations (1921–), the Trilateral Commission (1973–), and similar organizations.

The Wall Street Connection

Want to become unemployable at any university in the United States? Write *Wall Street and the Bolshevik Revolution*, and have it published by Arlington House, the conservative publishing company. Demonstrate that the "kook" theory that New York bankers and big business leaders financed the Bolshevik revolution is really not so far off base. Name those businessmen who actually did it. Show why they did: to win lucrative trade monopolies with the new Communist government. Show that Lenin paid off, and that his successors did and still do.

Then write *Wall Street and FDR*. Have Arlington House publish that, too. Show that Franklin Roosevelt began his career as a lawyer with the law firm whose principle client was the New York banking firm of J. P. Morgan. Show that he got his first appointment in government, as Assistant Secretary of the Navy, because of the intervention of Morgan partner Thomas W. Lamont. Show that after his ill-fated candidacy for Vice President in 1920, he became vice president of something else: Fidelity &

Deposit Insurance Co. of Maryland, and resident director of the company's New York office. Franklin Roosevelt was on the board of directors of eleven corporations, the president of a large trade association, and a partner in two law firms, 1921–28. Show that, by profession, FDR was a banker and an international speculator. Entitle Part III, "FDR and the Corporate Socialists."

Give an account of his relatives, who were also well-connected on Wall Street. FDR's favorite uncle, Frederic Delano, was appointed in 1916 by Woodrow Wilson to the Federal Reserve Board, and he was later chairman of the Federal Reserve Bank of Richmond (1931–36). He was the president of three railroads along the way.

Then go the whole nine yards. Write *Wall Street and the Rise of Hitler*. Even Arlington House won't touch that one. Get Gary Allen to publish it.

That, of course, is what Antony Sutton did. But why not? He was already unemployable in high-level academia. He was a judicious and remarkable scholar who wrote himself out of an academic career, despite (possibly because of) the erudition of his performance in *Western Technology and Soviet Economic Development* (3 volumes, Hoover Institution Press), which shows that 95% of all Soviet technology had been imported from, or stolen from, the West, 1917–1967. Because of what he discovered when writing this academic study, he concluded that the Soviet Union must have purchased most of its military technology from the West, too.

He then made the mistake of publishing this conclusion, along with the evidence, in a popular form through a conservative publishing house: *National Suicide* (Arlington House, 1973). He demonstrated beyond any shadow of a doubt that profit-seeking U.S. firms have gotten rich by selling the Soviet Union the military technology that alone made it a credible threat to the West. One doesn't voice such embarrassing conclusions to "the conservative rabble" if one is on the staff of the Hoover

Institution, a *respectable* conservative Establishment think-tank. So he got fired. (Amazingly, Harvard University's distinguished historian and Sovietologist, Richard Pipes, acknowledged in his book, *Survival Is Not Enough*, that Sutton's thesis regarding the Western origins of Soviet technology is essentially correct, and he also admitted in a footnote that the academic world has deliberately ignored Sutton's three-volume work because his conclusions embarrassed them. This admission came about a dozen years too late for Sutton's academic career.)[3]

Well, then, why not blow the whole career deal? Once blown, Sutton *really* took the plunge: with a book on "The Order," which Sutton believes (though has not yet proved) is an international conspiracy.[4] Its one visible manifestation in the U.S. (as far as the evidence now indicates) is Skull and Bones, Yale's ancient secret society, which President George Bush (Council on Foreign Relations—resigned) and William F. Buckley, Jr. (C.F.R.) belong to. This thesis was too much even for Gary Allen. "I find it hard to believe," Allen told me, "that the conspiracy's control over America is ultimately determined by the Registrar at Yale University." Sutton got a newsletter publisher, Research Publications, to publish the initial versions of the book. Think of the challenge: "You, too, can become Gary Allen's Gary Allen." He did it. Fringe City.

What is my point? Simple. Any graduate student or untenured scholar who starts writing articles demonstrating how self-interested, super-rich groups have captured America's *liberal, democratic, and progressive* institutions, *and still control these institutions*, will find himself isolated and ultimately unemployed. If he is incorrect about the details of his thesis, he will be easily dismissed as a crank, and I do mean *dismissed*. If he is correct, and his case starts getting a hearing, those who set the climate

---

3. Richard Pipes, *Survival Is Not Enough: Soviet Realities and America's Future* (New York: Simon & Schuster, 1984), p. 290, footnote 29.

4. Antony C. Sutton, *America's Secret Establishment: An Introduction to The Order of Skull & Bones* (Billings, Montana: Liberty House, 1986).

of opinion need only make a few discreet phone calls, or publish a devastating review or two in prestigious academic journals. Such things as existing conspiracies that are successfully misleading the people are simply not supposed to be mentioned by prudent scholars. Heads, he loses; tails, he loses. Right or wrong about the conspiracy, he loses.

A Crucial Alliance

People with Ph.D.'s are not stupid people. Narrow-visioned, perhaps, but not stupid. They respond to sticks. They also respond to carrots. Carrots have been made available. A cozy relationship has grown up between "public-spirited" foundations—Rockefeller, Ford, Carnegie, etc.—and departments of history and social science at major graduate schools. That relationship is marked by the presence of "research fellowships." But we are not supposed to think of this arrangement as a form of bribery. No, it is simply the enlightened funding of much-needed scholarship.

Lest readers be skeptical of this accusation, be it noted that the Rockefeller Foundation's *Annual Report* in 1946 announced that it was going to give the Council on Foreign Relations $139,000 (1946 dollars!) to produce a history of the United States' entry into World War II. This assignment, which was subsequently written by Harvard historian William L. Langer, was designed to counter any "revisionist" histories that might argue that we were tricked into war by the Roosevelt Administration. The Council sought to avoid a repetition of the post-World War I episode in revisionism, when several highly successful academics demonstrated that the U.S. was tricked by Wilson into entering the War.[5]

---

5. Harry Elmer Barnes, *Genesis of the World War* (1926); C. Hartley Gratten, *Why We Fought* (1929); Walter Millis, *The Road to War: America, 1914–1917* (1935); Charles C. Tansill, *America Goes to War* (1938). See Warren I. Cohen, *The American Revisionists: The Lessons of Intervention in World War I* (Chicago: University of Chicago Press, 1967).

What I am saying is that *there is an alliance between professional historians and the manipulating Establishment.*[6] This alliance is not easily proven. The ties are elusive. But that, too, is to be expected. Successful conspiracies *are* elusive. No one issues direct orders to history departments or publishers. There may or may not be a C.F.R. member as chairman of the department. But there are unquestionably unwritten rules of the game. It is more like *etiquette* than anything else: there are standards of proper behavior, and people who consistently violate these standards just don't get invited to the really nice parties. Those who never attend nice parties don't get to meet important people, either.

There are few aspects of *successful* conspiratorial groups more important for both recruiting and control than people's desire to be in the presence of powerful and famous people. The C.F.R. uses this weakness of men—and it is a dangerous weakness—to manipulate local leaders and businessmen through regional World Affairs Council meetings. Entrance into the C.F.R. itself is very important as a motivating device. Once in, the road to the top (or is it the center?) becomes confusing. How, precisely, do people get chosen? And how are they initiated? This is an important theme in Lewis' novel, *That Hideous Strength.* In a little-known but important essay, "The Inner Ring," Lewis warned young men against the quest for what I call the "unholy grail" of the inner circle.[7]

Non-Profit Restrictions

Another factor is also very important. In non-profit institutions, performance is judged by one's peers, not by consumers,

---

6. Don Fisher, *Fundamental Development of the Social Sciences: Rockefeller Philanthropy and the United States Social Science Research Council* (Ann Arbor: University of Michigan Press, 1993). See also Barry D. Karl, *Charles E. Merriam and the Study of Politics* (Chicago: University of Chicago Press, 1974).

7. C. S. Lewis, "The Inner Ring," *The Weight of Glory and Other Addresses* (New York: Macmillan, 1980), pp. 93–105.

as it is in a free, competitive market. People who work for universities or foundations must please their peers and their immediate superiors. A person cannot prove his or her importance to the organization by pointing to the corporate profit-and-loss statement. There is no profit-and-loss statement in a non-profit organization. Thus, scholars are figuratively held captive by their peers. Ideological deviation in such an environment can be fatal to a career.

These people are usually petrified of the free market. They have spent all their lives in academic bureaucracies. The uncertainties of market competition scare them, which is why most of them work for comparatively little money (although they don't have to work very hard, either). They are psychologically tied to their jobs in a way that people in the business world are not. The tighter the academic job market—and it grew incredibly tight in 1969 and has remained so—the more fearful they are. They can imagine few employment alternatives outside their non-profit universe. Thus, a raised eyebrow from a superior, especially if an assistant professor has not received tenure—a legal guarantee of lifetime employment—can work wonders.

Something else must be understood. Advancement—either upward or outward (a better place of employment)—is essentially medieval. It is not what you know but *whom* you know. Especially in your first few jobs, you need the support and recommendations of senior professors. Personal recommendations are major screening devices for hiring. This is why people try to get into prestigious departments in graduate school: better-known senior professors have a wider group of contacts. Contacts are vital.

To make it into the academic "big time" in social science, you have to be an absolute genius, as well as someone who has a knack at writing articles for professional journals, or you have to have the right contacts. But few people are geniuses. Thus, contacts are probably 80% of the game for 80% of the players in the big time competition. (Yes, the same rule applies to the "hard" sciences like chemistry and physics, although the presence of jobs in private industry—free-market, profit-seeking firms—reduces the level of control. Consider: Who hands out the big money for research projects? The Federal government and private foundations.)

The manipulators offer young, aggressive, ambitious men the necessary contacts.

The Ethics of Babel

There is yet another factor which seals the alliance: *shared presuppositions*. The manipulators, like the academics, are usually ethical relativists. They believe that there are no permanent standards of national morality. There are only "interests." Interests are shifting and temporary. (And who is best equipped to interpret changing conditions, identify today's "true" national interests, and formulate the appropriate national policies? Guess who.)

Check the title of Robert Osgood's (C.F.R.) 40-year-old, but still in print college text, which defends our C.F.R.-controlled foreign policy: *Ideals and Self-Interest in America's Foreign Relations* (University of Chicago Press, 1953). You get the picture. The book's subtitle is also interesting: *The Great Transformation of the Twentieth Century*. Indeed, it was!

Don't these scholars at least understand that nations, like individuals, are marked by certain ultimate commitments? Don't they understand that there are fundamental principles that divide men permanently? Don't they understand that the story of the Tower of Babel really tells us a fundamental truth about the limits on men's ability and willingness to join together politically? No, they don't. There is only one overarching ethical premise for them, one which unifies all mankind: *the brotherhood of man*. This must eventually lead to a new *community of man*. It must lead to a New World Order.

What Osgood wanted was a New World Order, although this term was not in use in academic circles back in 1953. He wanted to see it established, however, in the name of what he thought should be (but obviously isn't) acceptable to good, realistic, pragmatic Americans, meaning people without fixed moral principles. Flexible people. Deal-doers, but of a very special variety. *Deal doers who do deals with our declared mortal enemies.* You know, the kind of people who sold repeating rifles to the Sioux Indians in 1875. When Custer got killed a year later, the salesmen no doubt blamed Custer for foolhardiness. No doubt today's generals would agree. They have learned from MacArthur's experience—and, indirectly, from Sing-laub's[8]—that critics of the foreign policy which is designed to assist the rifle salesmen don't survive either the Indian chiefs or their Commander-in-Chief. (Interesting, isn't it, that every Commandant of West Point for a generation has been a C.F.R. member?)[9]

In history and political science departments around the country, this commitment to *pragmatic flexibility* has also long been recognized as the highest moral ideal for nations. The manipulators and the academics share rhetoric because they share basic principles. Principle Number One: There are *no* ethical norms that inherently divide "the community of man." (Principle Number Two: don't go out of your way to aid the career of anyone who rejects Principle Number One, unless you are trying to work some sort of deal.) *Ethics without permanent norms!* Here is an ethical ideal dear to the hearts of pragma-tists—and also to thieves, traitors, and other skilled profession-als in search of new victims. Osgood writes:

> Idealists must recognize as a basic condition for the realization of
> the liberal and humane values the creation of a brotherhood of

---

8. Major General John Singlaub protested once too often against Jimmy Carter's announced intention to pull U.S. troops out of South Korea. Singlaub's career ended, but the troops stayed.

9. Susan Huck, "Lost Valor," *American Opinion* (October 1977); "Military," *American Opinion* (July/August 1980).

mankind in which all men, regardless of physiological, social, religious, or political distinctions, will have equal partnership and in which human conflicts will be settled by reason, morality, and law rather than by physical power, coercion, or violence. And idealists must seek, as an integral part of this brotherhood, a progressive command over nature, to the end that every individual may share the material benefits essential to a full and happy existence on earth" (pp. 6–7).

In short, dig down deep into your wallet, American taxpayer: you owe it to the world. And by the way, you also owe your country to the world:

The pursuit of a universal goal may demand the practice of that extreme form of idealism, national altruism, according to which men dedicate themselves to the welfare of other nations and peoples without regard for their own nation's welfare. But the ultimate form of idealism is national self-sacrifice, which demands the deliberate surrender of one's own nation's self-interest for the sake of other nations and peoples or for the sake of some moral principle or universal goal. Every ideal demands that nations place some restraints upon egoism and renounce the more extreme forms of self-interest, but the ideal of self-sacrifice must countenance even the surrender of national survival itself (p. 7).

Feed this one-world drivel to a generation of college students, and you have sown the seeds of surrender within the next generation's educated elite. You have also screened the next generation of college teachers.

The universal goal is "the brotherhood of man." (You remember the first great demonstration of the brotherhood of man, don't you? Cain killed Abel.) Nelson Rockefeller used the phrase "brotherhood of man, fatherhood of God" so often that reporters invented an acronym for it: *bomfog*.[10] Thus, conven-

---

10. "In Rockefeller's Shadow," *The Economist* (April 6, 1996), p. 34.

tional liberal historians deny the operating principle of those who hold a conspiracy view of history, namely, that there *is* a continuing war between good and evil, between good men and bad men, and (if you happen to believe in a literal Bible) between good angels and fallen angels (demons). Having denied such a world view, "true" scholars can then all agree: the conspiracy view of history is infantile. They can all applaud David Rockefeller's letter to the editor to the *New York Times* (August 25, 1980), which begins: "I never cease to be amazed at those few among us who spot a conspiracy under every rock, a cabal in every corner." And we know who conspiracy theorists are! They are people who might dare to disagree with Rockefeller's conclusion in his letter:

> My point is that far from being a coterie of international conspirators with designs on covertly conquering the world, the Trilateral Commission is, in reality, a group of concerned citizens interested in identifying and clarifying problems facing the world and in fostering greater understanding and cooperation among international allies.

This sounds like a public relations bulletin from the League of Women Voters. (Would you deposit your life savings in a bank whose president writes like this?) "Concerned citizens . . . clarifying problems . . . greater understanding." You can almost hear the committee that must have edited this letter getting the giggles. You can almost see them nudging each other in the ribs and guffawing. "That ought to silence the rubes!" somebody blurts out. Yes, it ought to. The rubes who regularly read (and believe in) the *New York Times*.

The anti-conspiratorial perspective of most academic historians obviously works to the advantage of conspirators. Let's face it, if voters believe in manipulators, it is much more likely that they will become alert to the ways by which conspirators are manipulating the public. This "ill-informed rabble" might take steps to reduce their vulnerability to the manipulators. Clearly, outraged rabble-rousing voters can fight a self-interested group of monopoly-seekers a lot easier than they can fight "the forces of production" or "the *Volk.*" (Have you ever heard that "the forces of production" have been convicted for having attempted to bribe a U.S. Senator?)

But once in a while, some bright inner circle member gets out of line. He just can't keep a secret any more. That is the trouble with scholars: their careers are made by discovering some new fact or other, and yet they are supposed to know when to keep certain facts secret. Sometimes they forget. It can be very embarrassing.

6

MAVERICK "INSIDER" HISTORIANS

And they came to Balaam, and said to him, Thus saith Balak the son of Zippor, Let nothing, I pray thee, hinder thee from coming unto me. For I will promote thee unto very great honour, and I will do whatsoever thou sayest unto me: come therefore, I pray thee, curse me this people. And Balaam answered and said unto the servants of Balak, If Balak would give me his house full of silver and gold, I cannot go beyond the word of the Lord my God, to do less or more (Numbers 22:16–18).

Balaam was a prophet. He was not a man of God, but he was a spokesman for God. He later was executed at Moses' command (Numbers 31:7–8) for the treachery which he had shown to Israel (Numbers 31:16). But in this earlier incident, he refused to prophecy falsely against the Israelites. Balak the king sought his counsel and his curse against Israel, but Balaam refused to co-operate.[1]

What was true of this "court" prophet is sometimes (though rarely) true of modern court historians. Despite the overwhelming unity of professional opinion against conspiracy theories (and theorists), from time to time a certified scholar breaks

---

1. Gary North, *Sanctions and Dominion: An Economic Commentary on Numbers* (Tyler, Texas: Institute for Christian Economics, 1996), ch. 13: "The Office of Court Prophet."

loose and publishes a book which demonstrates the power and influence of conspiracies in history. It is never clear what motivates a man to make such a break with conventional behavior. It could be professional pride. It could be anger at some perceived slight. It could be the desire to tell an interesting story that hasn't been told before. It could even be that the tale-teller doesn't initially perceive the damage he is doing to those who have successfully sought power. But for one reason or another, he blows the whistle.

Carroll Quigley

Such a book is Prof. Carroll Quigley's monumental (and unfootnoted) *Tragedy and Hope* (Macmillan, 1966). The authors of *None Dare Call It Conspiracy* relied heavily on it. Macmillan decided not to reprint it after 1968, even though its sales were accelerating. But this is normal; book publishers often cease publishing fat, expensive books that cost a fortune to typeset, just as these books begin to sell well. As mid-1950's T.V. comic George Goebel used to say, "Suuuure they do."

Don Bell, a conservative newsletter publisher, came across a copy of the book in 1966 and alerted his readers to its importance. Word began to spread. Macmillan then killed it. Quigley's earlier manuscript, later titled *The Anglo-American Establishment*, was written in the late 1940's. It was not published until 1981. It is devoted to the British connections; it barely mentions the American establishment. *Tragedy and Hope* for years has been available only in a so-called "pirate" edition.

Quigley, who died in 1977, was professor of history at Georgetown University's prestigious School of Foreign Service, and was rightly regarded (especially by Quigley) as the most brilliant faculty member in the department. He taught President Clinton history, which Clinton mentioned in his 1992 acceptance speech at the Democratic National Convention. But be it noted: Quigley did not publish any of his findings about the conspiracy until very late in his career, and only because members had turned files over to him (he later claimed). In fact, he published only one minor, obscure, and totally harmless book prior to *Tragedy and Hope*.[2] Was he brilliant? Unquestionably. Judicious? Unquestionably. He built his early career in terms of the first principle announced in Proverbs 12:23: "A prudent man concealeth knowledge."

Tragedy and Hope is not all juicy conspiratorial material. Most of it is straight diplomatic, political, and economic history. All of it is brilliant. His insights on such otherwise ignored (and crucially important) topics as Japanese military history and its relation to family dynasties is fascinating. But it did not gain its notoriety or its sales because of these non-conspiratorial insights.

Why did Macmillan publish it? If they were unwilling to reprint the book after it was published, why publish it in the first place? It is quite possible that it got by a team of editors by mistake. After all, probably 98% of the book looks conventional. It has no footnotes, so it looks like a textbook, and few textbooks ever reveal anything unconventional. Furthermore, the Preface looks positively naive. He predicted the dwindling of the Cold War after 1962, and proclaimed "the growing parallelism of the Soviet Union and the United States, and the growing emphasis in all parts of the world on problems of living standards, of social maladjustments, and of mental health, replacing the previous emphasis on armaments, nuclear tensions, and heavy industrialization." This was standard liberal pabulum in 1965. In fact, it was substandard pabulum; in 1965 the Vietnam war was escalating. The head of Macmillan could not read every book manuscript in advance, especially one so huge that it becomes a 1300-page book. This one probably slipped through the cracks. (This was my conclusion before I spoke

---

2. *The Evolution of Civilizations: An Introduction to Historical Analysis* (Indianapolis, Indiana: Liberty Press, [1961] 1979). Ironically, it is published by a libertarian publishing house which is neither conservative nor modern liberal.

with Gary Allen and Cleon Skousen, who concluded the same thing.)

These mistakes do happen. For example, Otto Scott, a profound but unfortunately little-known conservative journalist-author (the man who coined the phrase, "the silent majority"), had his sensational book on John Brown published by Times Books, a subsidiary of the *New York Times*. *The Secret Six* reveals the details of the conspiracy of Unitarian ministers behind the murderous John Brown in the 1850's.[3] *The Secret Six* hit the book stores in 1980. Then, according to Scott, the company lost any interest in promoting it. (This is putting Scott's version as mildly as I can.) He bought back the publishing rights and all of the remaining copies later that year.

A similar case, according to legal scholar Henry Manne (MANee], happened to him when a pro-free-market book of his got into print, and it subsequently outraged a senior official in the publishing company, who told Manne face to face that he intended to kill it. That book, too, created a minor sensation, but in the economics profession and scholarly legal circles. This was not the intention of the publisher, although it had been Manne's intention.

Tragedy and Hope was published two years before the conservatives began getting excited about it. It initially set no sales records. Don Bell (of *Don Bell Reports*) stumbled upon that single copy in 1966 and featured it in one of his newsletters, but not many people paid any attention. Word began to get out by 1968. It began to be quoted by Gary Allen in *American Opinion*, the John Birch Society magazine, beginning in early 1969. Then Cleon Skousen published *The Naked Capitalist* in 1970. This book was basically a compilation of excerpts of Quigley's

---

3. R. J. Rushdoony had written about the Secret Six in 1965, but few people have ever read his chapter on "The Religion of Humanity" in his low-selling little classic, *The Nature of the American System*, which was published by a small religious publishing firm, the Craig Press.

book. By 1985, it had sold over a million copies; the first half million came by 1973. *None Dare* came out in 1972.

Sales of *Tragedy and Hope* began to take off in 1968, but supplies of the book ran out, and Macmillan declined to reprint it. They also destroyed the plates, according to author Quigley. I know one man who paid $150 for a used copy, so tight was supply, before a "pirate" edition appeared around 1975. (The publishers agreed to pay a royalty to Quigley, so it is more of an "unsuppressed book" than a true pirate edition.) Here is Prof. Quigley's account of what he alleged was the suppression of *Tragedy and Hope*:

> The original edition published by Macmillan in 1966 sold about 8800 copies and sales were picking up in 1968 when they "ran out of stock," as they told me (but in 1974, when I went after them with a lawyer, they told me that they had destroyed the plates in 1968). They lied to me for six years, telling me that they would re-print when they got 2000 orders, which could never happen because they told anyone who asked that it was out of print and would not be reprinted. They denied this until I sent them xerox copies of such replies to libraries, at which they told me it was a clerk's error. In other words they lied to me but prevented me from regaining the publication rights by doing so (on OP [out of print] rights revert to holder of copyright, but on OS [out of stock] they do not.) . . . Powerful influences in this country want me, or at least my work, suppressed.[4]

Several years before Quigley wrote this letter, Larry Abraham and Gary Allen appeared on a radio talk show where the interviewer had scheduled Quigley to debate with them over the phone. Quigley immediately denied that he had written the sensational material that Abraham and Allen had attributed to him. As soon as Abraham read one of the denied passages over

---

4. Letter to Peter Sutherland, December 9, 1975; reprinted in *Conspiracy Digest* (Summer 1976), and reprinted again in *American Opinion* (April 1983), p. 29.

the air, reading directly from Quigley's book, Quigley hung up. Elapsed time: less than two minutes. So much for extended scholarly debate.

It seems clear in retrospect that Quigley never expected the book to become *the* source of ammunition for the conservatives, nor did Macmillan. I doubt that Quigley knew what he was getting into when he began the project in the mid-1940's, when he started doing the research. That Macmillan refused to reprint it indicates outside pressure. The book was a mistake from the perspective of those exposed. Whatever their motives for allowing him access to documentary material (which he claimed that they had),[5] they later changed their minds about the wisdom of this. Or perhaps they never expected him to write a book using their materials. After all, he had never published anything controversial before, and it was late in his academic career.

In the late 1970's, Gary Allen received an unsigned letter. The envelope was postmarked "Washington, D.C." I have seen it and the envelope. The sender said that he had been a friend of Quigley's, and that at the end of his life, Quigley had concluded that the people he had dealt with in the book were not really public benefactors, as he had believed when he wrote it. According to the anonymous writer, Quigley had come to think of them in the same way that Allen did, and that Quigley had been very fearful of reprisals toward the end of his life. I believe the letter-writer.

James Billington

Quigley's scholarship was matched by James Billington's account of revolutionary movements in the period 1789 through 1917. Billington's *Fire in the Minds of Men: Origins of the Revolutionary Faith* (Basic Books, 1980) is nothing short of a master-

---

5. Carroll Quigley, *Tragedy and Hope: A History of the World in Our Time* (New York: Macmillan, 1966), p. 950.

piece. It is one of those exceedingly rare books which is simultaneously seminal and seemingly definitive—not just a pathbreaker, but a four-lane highway. It is a standing testimony to the failure of all previous, certified, Establishment scholars to take seriously the role of conspiracies in European history. Furthermore, while Quigley almost never provided footnotes (though there are a lot of them in *Anglo-American Establishment*), Billington buries the reader in footnotes, in more languages than any of us cares to learn, and from more obscure books and scholarly journals than any of us cares to know about. The silence from the historical profession has been deafening. (The same silence also greeted volumes two and three of Antony Sutton's previously mentioned three-volume bombshell, *Western Technology and Soviet Economic Development*.) What they cannot answer, professional historians prefer to ignore.

Billington focuses on the revolutionary underground: secret societies, pornographers, occultists, and revolutionary journalists, who established the basic philosophy and organizational structure of the twentieth century's bloody revolutionary groups. What he shows is that the "rational" socialists and revolutionaries of the "left" were from the beginning deeply mixed up in such things as occultism, irrationalism, and pornography. He exposes the dark side of "progressive" revolutionary forces.

He does not discuss events after 1917, nor does he provide much material that would link today's Establishment manipulators (or their spiritual forebears) to revolutionary movements. What he does do, however, is to demonstrate that twentieth-century Marxism and socialism were born in dubious circumstances. Without support from the occult underground and what income and influence the founders derived from service as popular journalists, there would have been no "inevitable victory of the proletariat," no "vanguard of the revolution."

Billington had previously been a Harvard and Princeton history professor, and is a C.F.R. member. Today, he is the Librarian of Congress. By all standards, he is one of the highest-level academic "insiders." They still remember Quigley, whose book discussed the Establishment groups that have financed such revolutionary groups, and that have used and misused portions of this revolutionary ideology to further their own ends. Billington did not write a Quigley-type book, but it turned out to be a spectacular account of the organizational roots of modern revolutionism.

PhD? What is still needed is a comprehensively researched fusion of these two approaches which demonstrates the existence of a continuing alliance of the revolutionary underground and the Establishment. With footnotes. Or as Allen and Abraham wrote in *None Dare*, pressure from below combined with pressure from above, "a dictatorship of the elite disguised as a dictatorship of the proletariat."

This is not to say that Billington was unaware of this alliance. He does not pursue the topic, but his book begins with the most important of all these alliances historically, the alliance between alienated segments of the French nobility (especially the King's cousin, Philip of Orléans) and the perverts of the Parisian underground. Philip gave them legal and geographical sanctuary and a forum for their ideas in the gigantic garden spot in central Paris, which he controlled, the Palais-Royal. As Billington remarks, "Nowhere—the literal meaning of Utopia— first became someplace in the Palais-Royal" (p. 25). He makes it clear that the Parisian mob was the tool of this alliance, not an independent force in the coming of the French Revolution. The French Revolution and the Russian Revolution were not the product of impersonal forces of history. They were the product of long years of conscious conspiratorial organization and planning. This is not your standard textbook account.

The Hole in the Ship

There is a familiar progression in the responses of those who are faced with the growing popularity of some heretofore objectionable idea. It goes something like this:

Stage one: "It isn't true."
Stage two: "It's true, but it's irrelevant."
Stage three: "We knew all about it years ago."

Step by step, younger scholars are breaking new ground, and those who once controlled access to the documentary records, and who sat on the editorial committees of the major publishing houses, are dying or retiring. The standard interpretations are beginning to change. For example, in discussing the entry of the United States into World War II, younger historians no longer say, "It isn't true" when the evidence of F.D.R.'s manipulating the nation into war is presented. We are at stage two, "It isn't relevant." In short, he needed to do it, and it was morally proper. When this story gets into the textbooks, as it eventually will, those who categorically denied it will all be dead, and younger men will say, "We always knew that."

What the conservatives have been reading since 1970 in their "unprofessional" little books and magazines is now being considered by scholars as possible explanations. Their language is less inflammatory, and their footnotes are different, but very bright men are coming to similar conclusions about "the way the world works." This development is what the conspirators have to reckon with today. If ever they are perceived as the losers, the historians will show them as little mercy as they have shown Hitler, another loser. Relativism-pragmatism has its risks. These risks are increasing daily.

And when you consider that millions of young people have been pulled out of the public schools and are being assigned textbooks that are not state-approved, you get some idea of the threat to the present system. Lose control of the next generation's educational materials, and a conspiracy is in deep trouble. They need legitimacy, and a lot of younger people are being prepared to revoke that legitimacy. The findings of the maverick historians serve as acids in the ship-of-state's hull.

7

THE SHIFT IN THE
CLIMATE OF OPINION

And the eyes of them that see shall not be dim, and the ears of them that hear shall hearken. The heart also of the rash shall understand knowledge, and the tongue of the stammerers shall be ready to speak plainly. The vile person shall no more be called liberal, nor the churl said to be bountiful. For the vile person will speak villany, and his heart will work iniquity, to practice hypocrisy, and to utter error against the Lord, to make empty the soul of the hungry, and he will cause the drink of the thirsty to fail (Isaiah 32:3–6).

The manipulators are in trouble—the worst trouble they have been in since 1913. Voters are at last figuring out that there are people in very high places who do vile things by means of liberal rhetoric. A growing minority of conservative Christian people are at last willing to call churls "churls." *The climate of opinion is shifting.* There is very little the Establishment can do about it. The seventy-year romance between the American voter and big government is turning into a series of lovers' quarrels. While the voters still want the government to protect them, and they still want the rich to pay "their fair share," there is a growing realization that the Federal government is bankrupt—economically, intellectually, and above all, morally.

The rise of the neo-conservative movement since 1965 is one indication of this shift. A lot of articulate New York Jews are not 1930's Trotskyites any longer; they are defenders of at least a modified free market, and they were vociferous critics of Communism of all varieties.

Let me give you a choice example. Midge Decter is the wife of Norman Podhoretz, the former editor of the highly literate neo-conservative magazine, *Commentary*, published by the American Jewish Committee. In one 12-month period, 1980–81, Decter, as an editor of Basic Books, oversaw the publication of four crucially important books: black ex-Marxist economist Thomas Sowell's *Knowledge and Decisions*, James Billington's *Fire in the Minds of Men*, conservative sociologist-historian Robert Nisbet's *History of the Idea of Progress*, and George Gilder's devastating criticism of the government welfare system, *Wealth and Poverty*. (Gilder was helped as a young man by David Rockefeller, who financed Gilder's Harvard education. This investment is now paying off for the conservatives, especially with Gilder's 1984 book, *The Spirit of Enterprise* [Simon & Schuster], an anti-bureaucracy, pro-entrepreneurship study.) I know of no other comparably stupendous year of editing in conservative book-publishing history. The climate of opinion is changing.

Singing a New Tune

All over the landscape these days, intellectuals are singing the praises of decentralization. New Age mystics, former Marxists, best-selling books like Alvin Toffler's *The Third Wave* and John Naisbett's *Megatrends* have all joined the chorus: a new day is a-comin'. Out with central planning, in with local decision-making.

The manipulators are trying to join in the song fest, but it's like dressing a Russian dancing bear in ballet shoes and calling it the Bolshoi's prima ballerina. They just can't pull it off. "Decentralization" is our program, and has always been our side of the debate. I think they are faking it; they still know that they have to have centralized power to maintain their power. They are not ready to decentralize anything they now control. But if they are forced to decentralize, they want to be able to say what and how far. They still want to run the show.

On the other hand, the shift of public opinion may be so powerful that some of them are actually defecting, especially the younger scholarly types. If this continues, today's power elite is headed for the dustbin of history (to use Trotsky's phrase).

They successfully used the pro-government shift in the American climate of opinion after, say, 1890 to further their statist ends. Now that the public has seen the results of this experiment in government centralization, voters are having second thoughts. The old faith in the government as planner is fading. The manipulators are now beginning to swim upstream intellectually, the way conservatives were forced to swim for three or four generations. The manipulators are not used to swimming upstream. They are out of shape. They are used to manipulating public opinion, not fighting it. They are skilled at "going with the flow," not getting swamped by it. They are desperately worried about the growing possibility of finding themselves up liberty creek without a paddle.

They always believe that they can make a deal. Now, sensing that the climate of opinion is shifting, they are tentatively starting to "buy in" to the new right movement. Chase Manhattan Bank in 1983 gave $50,000 to the Heritage Foundation, $15,000 to the Institute for Contemporary Studies, $40,000 to Manhattan Institute for Public Policy, and $10,000 to $20,000 each to several other conservative "public policy" foundations.[1] The C.F.R.'s magazine, *Foreign Affairs*, devoted a special issue in early 1985 to "America and the World, 1984." The editor opened it to some conservative critics such as Podhoretz.

---

1. *Conservative Manifesto* (February 1985), p. 6.

Why? Because they are opportunists by conviction and wind-testers by training. They understand that the pragmatist's question, "Does it work?" is being answered in the negative, in case after welfare case. The conservatives, especially the neo-conservatives, may not be offering consistent, free market, Constitutional solutions in many instances, but that is not the issue. The issue is, why have intellectuals begun to question the "tried and true" New Deal-Great Society answers? Why are these intellectuals critics at last announcing: "tried and *false*" solutions?

The answer sends chills down the spines of the manipulators: *because the statist solutions that they recommended, and they have long used to create their insulated, government-protected world, are visibly failing.* As the public, through new intellectual leadership, catches on, the power base of the conspirators will be threatened.

These people are really not that smart. After all, these are the people who, after seventy years, finally got their very own hand-picked man to be President of the United States, and it turned out to be grinning Jimmy, with his beer-loving brother (a paid Libyan agent), his evangelist sister (a pornographer's spiritual counsellor)—the President who produced simultaneously the worst foreign policy record in decades (including Salt II, which even the liberal, Democrat-controlled Senate refused to sign), and the most inflationary economic policy in peacetime U.S. history. In short, Jimmy ("Why not the Best?") Carter was visibly the least competent President in U.S. history.

It doesn't build up a conspirator's self-confidence, does it? This, in my view, is the heart of the matter. *The conspirators are losing self-confidence.* That is always the beginning of the end: in business, in politics, and in conspiracy. They are now on the run. The emperor has no clothes. Do you a hear a grinding, rasping sound? That's the Trilateral Commission scraping the bottom of the barrel. I smell fear. What should be our response? Attack!

Desperation Moves

I wrote the following in 1983:

What are the two forms of conspiracy likely to do over the next decade or so? The Communists will do what they have always done: intimidate the West, destabilize Third World nations, shout "boo!" to Western Europe whenever possible, take as few risks as possible, but steadily advance to cut off the West's "choke points": those 14 or 15 key shipping lanes for international commerce. These include the Persian gulf and southern Africa, as well as the Caribbean and the Panama Canal. They will nip at the heels of the U.S., always probing for weakness. They will find lots of weaknesses. They will continue to pressure the U.S. to abandon a space-based defense system. And step by step, the Soviet empire will grow too big to govern, even by means of terror, and too complex to finance, even by means of Western loans and stolen Western property.

The Establishment conspirators will do their best to keep people calm with respect to the solvency of the big banks, and keep them worried about the solvency of the economy in general. They need more power. They need more control over the private decisions of individuals. They will try to scare the public into granting them what they want. *We can expect to see a steady loss of confidence on the part of the public concerning political and economic leaders. We can also expect to see the imposition of emergency economic controls as the economy unravels.*[2] The dollar will eventually tumble, throwing the world trading economy into a crisis. The answer will be the same three-point program of Keynesians and liberals everywhere: taxation, regulation, and inflation.

I see no reason to modify what I wrote then, nor the sections that followed. The government's bills will come due. There will be a default when they do.

---

2. Gary North, *Government By Emergency* (Ft. Worth, Texas: American Bureau of Economic Research, 1983). On this point, so far, I was wrong.

A New Constitution

They would like to get a new Constitution to accomplish their goals. If voters can be frightened into allowing a Constitutional convention or similar event, the Establishment will shove a new Constitution down our throats. One very possible excuse: a wave of Latin American refugees streaming across the border, and having children who automatically become U.S. citizens. Racial and national feelings could easily be fanned into flames that could consume historic U.S. liberties.

If they are successful in revising the Constitution, then the most important asset they have enjoyed will be lost: voluntary co-operation (self-restraint) on the part of law-abiding Americans. Honest people will learn how to cheat dishonest civil government. They will learn how to beat the system. *If* we can successfully implement a two-part program of reconstruction, then this shift in psychology will destroy the prevailing conspiracy. If we don't implement it, a dark age will begin. The anti-utopias of George Orwell and Aldous Huxley will at last be imposed. I think we will implement our program.

Counter-Offensive

What we need is the will to resist. What we also need is a will to remove those from power over us who do not possess the will to resist, and whose very "let's make a deal" philosophy prevents them from ever resisting a truly dedicated force.

The first step is *self-education*. The next step is a program of education and mobilization—a morally grounded campaign—*from the bottom up*, to remove those above us who believe in a top-down control over society.

The conspirators in this nation have sought to overcome the free market with special-interest legislation—government-created monopolies—it thereby reveals the most important institutional tactic that can overcome *all* conspiracies: the limitation of civil government to its Constitutional role as defender of the peace. The civil government is not to save mankind; it is to protect residents from fraud and violence (domestic and international). But the State, in attempting to do more than this, has done less. We are no longer safe on the streets, precisely because the resources of the State have been misdirected into salvationary projects. Lyndon Johnson's use of Graham Wallas' ghastly phrase, "the Great Society," illustrates the lure of political messianism. From Teddy Roosevelt's Square Deal, to Woodrow Wilson's New Freedom, to Franklin Roosevelt's New Deal, to Harry Truman's Fair Deal, it has all been one basic movement: *the Raw Deal*. Raw for taxpayers, entrepreneurs, and freedom-lovers; beneficial for the manipulators.

There is only one way to deal with all forms of "conspiracy by manipulation": *cut off their funds*. Cut off their grants of State privilege. Exposure is not enough. They can live with exposure, though not so easily as without it. But they cannot live without the grants of State power that secure them from the competitive market economy—from the nipping at their heels by brighter, more innovative, and leaner competitors.

It is a wasted effort if we cut off the head of any conspiracy, but leave available to their replacements the raw power of the State, especially the centralized State. Like the hydra-headed monster of Greek mythology, for every head cut off, two more will spring up from the stump. The searing sword of economic liberty must be used to cauterize the monster's open wound and seal it. No more government-guaranteed loans, no more tariffs, no more import quotas, no more racial hiring quotas, no more price supports, no more minimum wage laws, no more compulsory union membership, no more graduated income taxes, and no more fractional reserve banking.

Above all, no more fractional reserve banking.

In short, the primary *public* institutional counter-offensive to all conspiracies is a civil government which is governed by this fundamental truth: *there is no such thing as a free lunch*. Or to put it bluntly, "You get your hand out of my wallet, and I'll get my hand out of yours." Until the vast majority of voters believe this, and vote in terms of it, conspirators will continue to manipulate the public effectively, and their hands will never get out of our wallets, for they will always tell each of us individually that they are digging even deeper into our neighbor's wallet, and besides, "it's in the public interest."

The Question of Faith

The second step after self-education is also primarily internal, though partially institutional. It is the response of faith. It is our acceptance of the principle that ethics is more fundamental than power, that the good guys win in the end.

I quoted the opening lines of Psalm 2 at the beginning of Chapter One. Now let me quote its conclusion. It warns rulers against becoming conspirators against God and God's law:

> Ask of me, and I shall give thee the heathen for thine inheritance, and the uttermost parts of the earth for thy possession. Thou shalt break them with a rod of iron; thou shalt dash them in pieces like a potter's vessel. Be wise now therefore, O ye kings: be instructed, ye judges of the earth. Serve the LORD with fear, and rejoice with trembling. Kiss the Son, lest he be angry, and ye perish from the way, when his wrath is kindled but a little. Blessed are all they that put their trust in him (Psalm 2:8–12).

This should be the ultimate hope of man. This is the foundation upon which societies must build. If you are not building in terms of this foundation, then a mountain of fully documented books on the Conspiracy will do you precious little good. Conspiracy books offer us shovels with which to bury the plans of evil men. They are not to be used to dig our own graves. As God said to Joshua after the death of Moses, and just before the invasion of Canaan,

Be strong, and of a good courage: for unto this people shalt thou divide for an inheritance the land, which I sware unto their fathers to give them. Only be strong and very courageous, that thou mayest observe to do according to all the law, which Moses my servant commanded thee: turn not from it to the right hand or to the left, that thou mayest prosper whithersoever thou goest (Joshua 1:6–7).

8

REPLACING EVIL WITH GOOD

And Jesus came and spake unto them, saying, All power is given unto me in heaven and in earth (Matthew 28:18).

To put it briefly, the good guy has already won. If He is Lord of your life, in principle so have you.

What is the main problem we face? Conspiracies? No. The real problem is the *set of moral, intellectual, and economic ideas that the West's voters have accepted as valid that have led to their partial enslavement.* The conspirators use these false religious principles to control Western societies. These false principles include the following:

1. Mankind is essentially unified.
2. There are no conflicting moral issues that divide people permanently.
3. Man must "take control" of man.
4. Mankind will eventually evolve into a "higher species"—a "leap of being."
5. Elite planners can use the laws of evolution to speed up this evolutionary process.
6. Men can be saved through State legislation.

7.   Men can be saved through education.

8.   Ideology is irrelevant; only "interests" count.

9.   "Deprived" individuals are not personally responsible for their acts.

10.   The State is the primary welfare agency rather than the family.

11.   The State should redistribute wealth to benefit "the People."

12.   The State must protect inefficient producers from free market competition.

13.   The State must supervise education.

14.   We need to construct a one-State world in order to achieve peace, freedom, and prosperity.

When a majority of voters accept a majority of these premises, the triumph of one or another conspiratorial group is assured. It is by means of these man-worshipping, State-worshipping ideas that conspirators enlarge the power of civil government, and it is by the power of civil government that they rule. To attempt to remove the ruling conspiracies without first removing most people's confidence in these false ideas is about as useful an effort as a condemned man's switching from hanging to the firing squad. Jesus described the results of such a self-defeating "housecleaning":

> When the unclean spirit is gone out of a man, he walketh through dry places, seeking rest, and finding none. Then he saith, I will return into my house from whence I came out; and when he is come, he findeth it empty, swept, and garnished. Then goeth he, and taketh with himself seven other spirits more wicked than himself, and they enter in and dwell there. . . . (Matthew 12:43-45a).

The owner of the house is worse off than he was when he started. This is the legacy of all political revolutions that are not grounded in biblical principles of social order. Men "throw the rascals out," only to find that a worse gang of rascals has replaced the first one.

The Gnostic Heresy

The ancient gnostics believed that man is saved by secret knowledge. They believed that man needs to be liberated from this world of matter and elevated, through secret initiation and certain ascetic techniques, into the realm of spirit. Certain groups of contemporary "New Age" humanists hold a very similar viewpoint. Unfortunately, there are a lot of Christians and far too many "we must reveal the conspiracy" fanatics who have adopted a variation of this ancient heresy. Their "secret initiation" into knowledge about their enemies, whether their enemy is the devil (in the case of Christian investigators) or the conspiracy (in the case of radical conservatives or leftists) serves them as a psychological justification for doing nothing. They think that just knowing more and more about "the Conspiracy" relieves them from *doing* anything about it. Their endless studying is an excuse for their inactivity. They spend their time with other similarly minded people, enjoying the impotent luxury of exchanging secret phases and knowledge of secret things. They have imitated their enemies; they have created their own inner ring—a secret ring which knows all about their enemy's secret ring. They become hypnotized with "circles within circles." Their great spiritual enemy thereby removes them from the real fight.

A continuing theme in this book is that we are not saved by knowledge. We are also not saved by power. We are saved by grace through faith in Jesus Christ as Lord and Savior, because He was God's substitute sacrifice for sinful men. Christ's victory over Satan and sin is in principle our personal and corporate victory over Satan and sin, in every area of life, including politics. Christianity is the *dominion* religion. It is not the power religion, nor is it the escape religion.[1]

The first thing to recognize in this cosmic struggle is that those who seek power through manipulation or through execution have in principle lost the battle. They lost it almost 2,000 years ago. They hold power temporarily. Although they are accomplished power manipulators, power is not the issue; *ethics* is the issue. God and His law are the issue. "Some trust in chariots, and some in horses: but we will remember the name of the LORD our God" (Psalm 20:7). "The chariots of God are twenty thousand, even thousands of angels" (Psalm 68:17a).

Our opponents are not supermen. They are not the masters of history. They are the heads of multinational banks that have more bad loans on their books than they have equity capital. They are the heads of oil companies that face the possibility of an oil glut and a collapse of oil prices. They are the people who gave us Jimmy Carter. They are not so smart. Or better put, they are way too smart for their own good (and ours). In any case, it isn't a question of brain power; it is a question of *ethical standing before God the Judge.*

Second, our opponents believe in the power religion. They have become skilled at the capture and retention of power. It is their way of life. Thus, they will not be displaced easily. Reading books about the conspiracy will not displace them. Voting for their hand-picked Presidential candidates every four years will not displace them. We will not be delivered by books or Presidential races. We should not place false hope in programs that are futile, or even self-destructive.

Replacement, Not Simply Exposure

For the sake of argument, let us say that two possibilities lie ahead. The first is that a group of principled people who are

---

1. Gary North, *Moses and Pharaoh: Dominion Religion vs. Power Religion* (Tyler, Texas: Institute for Christian Economics, 1985), Introduction.

utterly ignorant of the conspiracy are in a position to replace each conspirator in whatever office or job that is presently held by conspirators. The second possibility is that this same principled group can gain almost perfect knowledge about every aspect of the conspiracy, but in doing so, they use up all of their spare time. Which would you prefer, ignorant victory or well-informed defeat?

You may respond, "no one can replace the conspirators who does not know all about them. Knowledge comes first." But does it? What did the people of Israel know about the gods of Canaan that governed the promised land? Not much. They were not supposed to know much about them, either; God forbade them from even mentioning the names of these gods (Exodus 23:13). Nevertheless, God led them to victory over these gods under Joshua.

What did the Apostles know about Roman law or Roman military tactics? Not much, but God defeated the Roman Empire and used His people to replace the older Roman leadership. Christians by the year 325 were the only group left in Rome which was sufficiently moral and sufficiently productive to take over the administration of the crumbling Empire. Yet they had been outcasts: persecuted, politically inexperienced outcasts. All they had was a moral vision. All they had was perseverance. All they had was God.

It is not knowledge which saves us. What saves us is grace. What saves a society is the covenantal faithfulness of its people.

Our job is not to "throw the rascals out" in one glorious national election. Our job is to replace them steadily by our own competence. God did not promise Moses that the Hebrews would conquer the Canaanites overnight. On the contrary, He promised to preserve the Canaanites until their day of judgment had come, city by city, year by year:

> I will send my fear before thee, and will destroy all the people to whom thou shalt come, and I will make all thine enemies

turn their backs unto thee. And I will send hornets before thee, which shall drive out the Hivite, the Canaanite, and the Hittite, from before thee. I will not drive them from before thee in one year; lest the land become desolate, and the beast of the field multiply against thee. By little and little I will drive them out from before thee, until thou hast increased, and inherit the land (Exodus 23:27–30).

God promised them victory. He promises us victory, too. But this victory is a slow, continual process. It is *victory through competence*. It is *victory through steady, long-term replacement*. We need the conspirators to "mind the land" while we are preparing ourselves for full-time, comprehensive biblical service. Never forget, we still have essentially a free market society. The conspirators have to make a living, just as we do. They also have to meet a market. They also have to serve the consumers in order to make a profit. The West's markets are only partially rigged. Government-created, government-protected monopolies are only marginally powerful in most cases. If the conspirators were to go on strike overnight in their capacity as economic producers, the whole economy would topple. We are not yet ready to lead, any more than the Israelites were in Moses' day. It is our job to prepare ourselves for competitive free market service in every area of life. If we do this, and do it diligently, our victory is assured. Until we do, a victory would only humiliate us.

What good has a 30-year program of exposure done so far? Hundreds of anti-conspiracy books were published, 1965-85, yet hardly one of them can be bought at any book store today, and very few are still in print. They were not suppressed by the conspirators; they were ignored by them. They were ignored by practically everyone else, too.

My point is simple: such books are curiosities, not solutions. They have led in the past to paralysis. Only *a positive program of self-conscious Christian reconstruction* can counter the power and influence of the conspirators. Only a comprehensive program based on good ideas can defeat an entrenched political order based on universally shared bad ideas. In short, *you can't beat something with nothing*. You have to fight something evil with something good.

What Is to Be Done?

This was the question Lenin asked in his famous pamphlet. It had been asked by Russian revolutionaries for a generation. A counter-offensive is called for. Not a defensive holding action. Not a retreat into the historical shadows. It must be a *bottom-up*, decentralized offensive campaign. The top-down, centralized strategy is the strategy of our opponents. What we need is a long-term grass roots campaign at every level of politics, economics, and institutional influence, in every region of the country—indeed, every region of the world.

This will happen when God's people faithfully begin to sacrifice for a long-term program of *comprehensive redemption*.[2] They must first assume that when God saves men's hearts, He intends thereby to save every area of life touched by redeemed men's hearts—every relationship and every institution. To aim at less is to default to the devil. To grant the devil a single square inch of legitimate authority is to capitulate in principle to his program. What we need is a four-fold program:

1. The will to ethics
2. The will to resist
3. The will to self-education
4. The will to dominion

We need to act righteously, whatever the cost, but do so on the basis of true knowledge, in order to roll back Satan's kingdom of illegitimate power.

---

2. Gary North, *Is the World Running Down? Crisis in the Christian Worldview* (Tyler, Texas: Institute for Christian Economics, 1988), Appendix C: "Comprehensive Redemption: A Theology for Social Action."

There are many books on the conspiracies of this world. What there has not been is a serious, long-term, multiple level, yet *decentralized* counter-offensive against the forces of evil. Conservative organizations have come and gone, but still the power-brokers remain entrenched in the seats of power. They still make deals with our mortal enemies. All the paperback exposés since 1961 have done nothing to roll back the illegitimate profits of the deal-doers. We are not saved by knowledge, nor are they particularly threatened by it. Paperback books will not dislodge them. A principled, long-term, ethics-based counter-offensive will dislodge them. Shrink the State!

[Written, remember, in 1985:] I propose a program. Some variant of this program must be adopted if we are to have any meaningful hope in recapturing the machinery of civil government, the media, and the educational institutions. It will be done. It has already begun. How long it will take is problematical; I think we will begin to see major victories before the year 2005. In two decades, our enemies will begin to feel the pressure; possibly sooner. They act as though they are on the offensive, but in fact they are already on the defensive. We need to be prepared to replace them in every area of life when the spiritual revival comes. This means that we need years of patient hard work in order to gain the experience we need to lead. There is no quick fix. We need the same kind of experience that David gained in the years that King Saul pursued him.

What I outline here is only an outline. Many steps are left out, and almost all the details. But something like this must develop if we are to preserve our declining freedoms.

Localism

You must start where you are. You must begin to take seriously the responsibilities God has assigned to you locally. "Think globally, work locally" is a biblical principle.

Church

Are you a member of a committed church? The "litmus tests" of serious Christian commitment for a church are two-fold:

1.   Does it operate (or support) a Christian day school?

2.   Is the pastor actively involved in the battle against abortion, including picketing abortion centers?

If the answer is "no" to both questions, try to get your church involved in these issues before you go to stage two, your program of anti-conspiratorial action. These are the first two programs that a church needs in a first-stage battle against any group of conspirators. If your church refuses to get involved in either project, find a new church. But do find one. This battle cannot be won alone. Radical individualism is the counsel of despair. This is a *covenantal fight* which will be won by covenantally faithful people. We are up against organized forces.

Let us assume that your church supports a Christian school and is actively involved in the fight against abortion. You now know who the "doers" are in the church—the people who are involved in the school and the fight against abortion. They have identified themselves. This is exactly what you need.

You need to join a local congregation that is doing something positive in the community. The church's officers should have a vision for making the community a better place to live. Maybe it offers marital counselling, or projects that help the poor. But it should be doing something.[3] It should not be sitting in the sidelines of life waiting for the Rapture.

---

3. Colonel V. Doner, *The Samaritan Strategy: A New Agenda for Christian Action* (Brentwood, Tennessee: Wolgemuth & Hyatt, 1988).

Family

Are your children enrolled in a private school? If not, stop worrying about some distant conspiracy. Anyone who gets himself in a dither about "the conspiracy this" or "the conspiracy that," but has not taken care to see that his children are in a humanism-free intellectual environment, is using his interest in the conspiracy deflect him from the important affairs of life. Until you cease "tithing your children" to the State, you are far too vulnerable to the enemy for you to begin a counter-offensive against him. You have turned your children's minds and environment over to the statist enemy. First things first: get them into a Christian school, or into a home school environment. Look in the Yellow Pages for the telephone numbers of local Christian schools or churches that operate schools.

If you cannot locate a good school, consider a home school curriculum. You would be amazed at how much an untrained mother can teach children, especially those under the sixth grade. There are many available curriculum materials, but two good programs are these:

> Covenant Home Curriculum
> 17700 W. Capitol Dr.
> Brookfield, WI 53045
>
> Christian Liberty Academy
> 502 W. Euclid Ave.
> Arlington Heights, IL 60004

Grandparents should offer to help subsidize tuition payments for their grandchildren. Forget about big annual Christmas expenditures. Buy the kids a few books each Christmas, and then help finance their attendance at a school which will teach them how to read them.

Have you seen to it that every teenager in your house has read this book, and other books on similar topics? What good does it do if your next door neighbor or some colleague at work reads and believes in this story, but your children go off to university never having heard anything about it? Are your children involved in summer reading or summer seminar programs?

A good two-week-long summer educational program for students age 16 or older is run by Rev. David Noebel. There is also a two-week course held at Bryan College, Dayton, Tennessee each summer. There are also a dozen one-week regional seminars for students age 13 and up.

Summit Ministries
P. O. Box 207
Manitou Springs, CO 80829
(719) 685-9103

There is also a one-year video program, *Understanding the Times*, which is in use in 750 Christian high schools. This parallels Dr. Noebel's book, *Understanding the Times* ($36.95).

Politics

The principle of localism is fundamental. It has been the suicidal urge of political conservatives to focus on the "big issues" at the national level, where their nearly invisible political opponents have long since mastered the art of deception. What we need is to develop skills on the local level before we can hope to defeat our opponents nationally. The county courthouse, the local school board, the city council: here are our initial targets.[4] If we cannot win here, why should we expect to

---

4. The goal of controlling the local public school board is not to make the public schools a good place for Christian students. Christian students should not be in tax-supported schools. The goal is to say "no" to every request by every teachers union, to say "no" to every liberal humanist textbook salesman, and to stop floating school bond proposals. The school board's job is to cut back on spending in every area, but especially the salaries of school administrators. It is also important to expel

win nationally? Is it pride which motivates good people with
minimal skills to seek the highest offices first? The biblical principle of authority is clear: success first in the family, then in the
church, then in civil and social affairs. Success in the little
things of life is to precede any attempts to master the big things
of life.

Where should the little person begin? Wherever he has
legitimate responsibility. After he has managed well here, he
can begin to think about increasing his authority. He must
resist at all costs a *premature grabbing of the robes of authority.* That
was Adam's sin. He just wouldn't wait.

Here is my recommended initial program of self-improve-
ment. It must precede other "more impressive" programs of
political reconstruction.

1. Prayer (personal and corporate)
2. Study (personal and corporate)
3. Local recruiting (evangelism)
4. Local confrontations (abortion, public
   schools, Planned Parenthood)
5. Creating newspaper clipping files for
   future reference
6. Continual monitoring of local elected
   representatives and board meetings
7. Continual monitoring of public school
   curriculum materials
8. Identifying local supporters or potential supporters on an issue-by-issue
   basis
9. Building a mailing list on an issue-
   by-issue basis

What kind of skills are involved? First and foremost, the
skills of long-term commitment and permanent self-discipline.

---

every delinquent on campus, including faculty members.

Only a minority of people possess such skills. This is why minorities always rule. This is why all institutions require representative government.

Second, there must be organizational skills. This may only be a willingness to put together a shoebox filing system that uses 3 by 5 inch note cards. It probably involves a willingness to buy an IBM PC clone with a gigabyte of hard disk and an introductory data base program, such as **Claris Works** or **Lotus Approach**. Claris Works has a very good word processing program and a spreadsheet built in. It is an all-in-one package. (So is Microsoft Works, but I like Claris Works better.)

Third, there must be personal communication skills. Any motivation and education program requires people who can speak to others face to face, hand out a newsletter, present a petition, invite to a meeting, etc. These may not be the organizers or the public speakers, but they are vital.

At the national level, two training programs stand out, the first for political candidates and campaign managers, and the second for college students.

Free Congress Foundation
721 Second St., N.E.
Washington, D.C. 20002

Leadership Institute
8001 Braddock Rd., Suite 502
Springfield, VA 22151

These political projects involve very specialized skills. Such skills are seldom possessed by any one person. A cooperative effort is called for. In short, Christian reconstruction necessarily involves *covenants*: family, church, and civil.[5] Success cannot come on the basis of pure individualism.

---

5. Ray Sutton, *That You May Prosper: Dominion By Covenant* (Tyler, Texas: Institute for Christian Economics, 1987).

Study Groups

You have read this book. You are convinced that something needs to be done. You may not be certain just what needs to be done, but you understand that the church needs to get involved. But what if your pastor is unaware of the material in this book? Give him a copy and ask him to evaluate it. See what he thinks. He may never have heard of any of this before.

On the other hand, he may know more about it than he lets on. He may know enough not to want to get involved. Almost no pastor ever wants to deal with these issues from the pulpit. It is risky. He may alienate some church members. If he were to preach about the problem, it would also require him to come up with concrete, biblical answers to the problems raised by this book. Very few pastors believe that the Bible really and truly speaks *specifically* to modern social, political, and economic questions. (Example: ask your pastor what the biblical criticism of the Federal Reserve System is. There is one.[6] Does he know what the answer is? Does he even know what the Federal Reserve System is? This is not the sort of question that most pastors seek answers to in the Bible.)

Furthermore, most pastors hold a pessimistic view of the future. They believe that Christian people will not be able to reverse the world's slide into chaos. They do not believe that God has a program of comprehensive redemption which is going to become visible across the earth *before* Jesus returns physically and ends history at the final judgment. Such an era of victory is what the Bible teaches.[7] Not many pastors believe this, however. Since they think Christians cannot win, they hesitate to get involved in a long-term battle against political

---

6. Gary North, *Honest Money: The Biblical Blueprint for Money and Banking* (Ft. Worth: Dominion Press, 1986). This is sold by the Institute for Christian Economics.

7. David Chilton, *Paradise Restored: A Biblical Theology of Dominion* (Ft. Worth, Texas: Dominion Press, 1985). Sold by the Institute for Christian Economics.

evil. Why get involved in a losing cause? They prefer to stay on the sidelines. It is safer to preach other kinds of sermons.

What can you do about this? Not much. You can set up a quiet study group for church members. I have outlined how students can do this on campus. You can imitate it. I include this very practical section in my highly controversial little paperback book, *75 Bible Questions Your Instructors Pray You Won't Ask: How to Spot Humanism in the Classroom or Pulpit*. You can order a copy for $5.95, plus a dollar for postage, from

Institute for Christian Economics
P. O. Box 8000
Tyler, TX 75711

To say that *75 Bible Questions* is controversial is an understatement. Pastors do not want their members reading such material. What if your pastor tells you to stop having study groups? You may choose to stop them, but you can still hand out copies of *Conspiracy: A Biblical View*—not to everyone (most people aren't ready for it), but to interested people. Let word of mouth tell the story. You need not become very visible if you choose not to.

You need to show considerable judgment in who you invite to investigate the problem of conspiracy. If someone in your church were dying of an incurable disease, would you rush to him and hand him a copy of this book? Is that what he needs at this point? Or what if there is some young couple which is having deep marital troubles. What if they are talking about divorce? Is their highest priority item a knowledge of conspiracies? What of the new convert, or the mentally disturbed person who is suffering from depression? Is that the person you are trying to recruit?

No, what you need is a stable person, someone who is in a position to take a leadership position some day. This is the kind of person that the conspirators try to recruit. So should you.

You need a person who reads, votes, donates his time and money to charities, takes his kids on vacation each year, and generally is a credit to God's kingdom. You should not be trying to recruit the walking wounded, the spiritual basket cases who wind up in the church. You need to be highly selective in recruiting people to the cause.

You need self-evaluation, too. Are you perceived as a "red hot"? Are you perceived as a loose loaded cannon rattling around on the deck? Are you noted for your temporary commitment to this or that cause to "save the world" – causes that usually fail, and which have yet to save the world? If so, you are a liability in the battle against conspiracies. Stay on the sidelines in this fight. Get involved in some other cause, such as bake sales or visiting the old folks home. You have to demonstrate that you are a worthy follower before anyone is going to believe that you are a potential leader. You need to "wait tables" for a few years, the way deacons should before becoming elders (Acts 6:2).

Conclusion

As anyone can see, there is a great deal to be done. There is therefore a great deal that anyone can do at several levels. Anyone who asks rhetorically, "But what can *I* do?" now has some very specific answers. This rhetorical question is not to become an excuse for inaction. *If you do nothing now, you have no excuse.*

Do I expect a flood of thousands of letters from dedicated people who have decided to get involved in one or more of the projects I have listed in this chapter? Of course not. Not one person in a hundred, if that, will respond by letter. But perhaps five or six per hundred who read this book will begin to do something, even though they never identify themselves by letter. Maybe a few hundred churches will at least begin to get involved in stage two, the stage beyond the Christian school fight and the abortion fight. If there is no response to the conspiracy's challenge, then the Spirit of God will pass over this generation just as surely as He passed over Moses' generation, which died in the wilderness. But if just a handful respond in our day, and adopt a vision of victory, then we will be as Joshua's generation: victorious on all fronts. God chooses the foolish of this world to confound the wise (I Corinthians 1:20). Gideon's experience proves that it only takes a handful of dedicated righteous people to achieve a victory.

So what about you? What will you do? At the very least, begin to monitor at least one of the special-interest groups of self-anointed elite planners. The Appendix gives you the names and addresses of several. Get on some mailing lists and see what they are up to. Find out who they are, too. Know your enemy. And then discipline yourself to become sufficiently efficient to replace him, at least at the local level.

CONCLUSION

If they shall confess their iniquity, and the iniquity of their fathers, with which they trespassed against me, and that also they have walked contrary unto me, and that I also have walked contrary unto them, and have brought them into the land of their enemies; if then their uncircumcised hearts be humbled, and they then accept of the punishment of their iniquity: then will I remember my covenant with Jacob, and also my covenant with Isaac, and also my covenant with Abraham; and I will remember the land (Leviticus 26:40–42).

The *will to ethics* is the first stage. If you will not act morally in terms of the information you have been given, then you are a bystander, and not an innocent bystander. Much is expected from those to whom much has been given (Luke 12:48).

The *will to resist* is the second stage. Satan and his host, both supernatural and earthly, have a strategy based on a myth: the sovereignty of anything except God. To persuade people of the validity of this myth, they have adopted the tactics of the power religion. They squash people who get in their way. Not everyone gets squashed—the enemies of God are not omnipotent, after all—but some people. They make it seem as though they can squash anyone and everyone, if they ever choose to do so. They use a combination of deception and terrorism to achieve their goals. Thus, the proper counter-measure is to learn the truth and to resist evil.

This decision must be made before getting involved in any long-term program of self-education; if it isn't, self-education can easily become an exercise in self-paralysis and eventual psychological escape. The more a partially committed person learns about the influence of the enemy, the more he grows convinced of the enemy's omnipotence. Too much insight into the workings of the opposition paralyzes weak investigators. This is why I seldom recommend that someone begin a detailed investigation of occultism; there ought to be a legitimate "need to know." One or two books on the topic should be sufficient, except for a prayerful specialist who needs more information for a particular task, not just information for its own sake. The "burned out" conservative who served as a discussion group leader for 15 years is a familiar casualty in the war.

When you get involved in anything, count the long-term costs. "For which of you, intending to build a tower, sitteth not down first, and counteth the cost, whether he hath sufficient to finish it? Lest haply [it happen], after he hath laid the foundation, and is not able to finish it, all that behold it begin to mock him, saying, This man began to build, and was not able to finish" (Luke 14:28–30).

The *will to self-education* is the third stage. The enemy has captured most of the tax-financed and non-profit educational institutions of our era. The enemy has also captured the major communications media: newspapers, book publishers, radio and television. They screen out facts that are uncongenial to their long-term goal of the political unification of mankind. Thus, truth-seekers are forced to find better information by means of "alternative media." Bible-preaching churches are the place to begin the search, but only a start. They, too, have been compromised. Their ministers and leaders have been educated in the enemy's schools and propagandized by the enemy's media. They, too, need to get involved in a self-education process. Only a minority are willing to do this. But at least they operate in terms of a manual of first principles which is at odds with the conspiracies: the Bible.

The *will to dominion* is the fourth—not the quest for power apart from ethical law, but the quest for authority by means of ethical action.[1] We need to do more than expose evil in high places. We need to make plans to *replace* evil in high places. You can't fight something with nothing.

This four-stage program, above all else, is what the conspirators fear, and cannot deal with successfully.

The Psychology of Defeat

The mentality of the anti-conspiratorialists has been a defensive mentality for seventy years. There has been a visible tendency for conservative people to shrivel up and die in the face of previously ignored and suppressed evidence concerning conspiracies. To some extent, this has been the fault of amateur conspiracy theorists, who have endeavored to prove their case by seeing all of history as a product of clever machinations by a single, unified, undivided conspiracy. These well-meaning people have adopted personalism, but not cosmic personalism. They have ignored God as *the* controlling factor in history. In some cases, they have begun to believe the far-out ravings of the occult fringe.

I think of one conspiracy theorist who has fortunately disappeared from view, and who never wrote a book, preferring to spread the word by means of seminars and audiocassette tapes. He was articulate, but at the end of his semi-public career (mid-1970's), he actually taught that the events of this world are controlled by about half a dozen "Tibetan masters" in the Himalayas. He took seriously the most nonsensical ravings of the New Age mystics. As Rushdoony once commented, such conspiracy theorists have believed in witchcraft to such a degree

---

1. Gary North, *Unconditional Surrender: God's Program for Victory* (3rd ed.; Tyler, Texas: Institute for Christian Economics, 1988).

that they think the witches are in control. In the name of fighting Satan, they have adopted his own bragging lies about himself. They have retreated from the fight.

What happens when a dedicated conspiracy-fighter begins to comprehend the power of the enemy? In a few cases, they may adopt the religion of the conspirators, the power religion. They switch sides. In most cases that I am familiar with, however, they merely have believed in the power religion's own propaganda, and they have grown fearful and despondent. They have dropped out of the fight. Perhaps they just stop reading about the Conspiracy, or politics in general. In one case that I am familiar with, the person adopted some sort of Eastern mystical religion and started having an annual sexual affair each summer vacation. In desperation, many have retreated into the escapist religion—a retreatist, pietistic, "God will Rapture me out of all this" religion. They have abandoned *orthodox* Christianity, the *ethics* religion, which is the *dominion* religion.[2]

Humble Before God, Fearless Before Men

The best defense is a good offense. We must take the offensive. And we must be governed by this vision: they are evil and will eventually lose; we are righteous and will eventually win. God is on our side. We are stronger than our enemies because we are right. Even if we personally do not win in our lifetimes, our successors who organize in terms of our principles will win.[3] Now is not the time for caution; the stakes are too high, and it is too late in the conflict.

Rushdoony's comments on the meaning of destiny and conspiracy need to be taken seriously:

---

2. Gary North, *Moses and Pharaoh: Dominion Religion vs. Power Religion* (Tyler, Texas: Institute for Christian Economics, 1985), Introduction.

3. David Chilton, *Paradise Restored: A Biblical Theology of Dominion* (Ft. Worth, Texas: Dominion Press, 1985). Sold through I.C.E.

The reluctance to call one's own position a conspiracy rests on the premise that destiny cannot be conspiracy; it is historical inevitability. Only that which seeks to conspire against destiny is conspiracy, which is some kind of desperate, dangerous and yet futile attempt to stay the clock of history. And, in a very real sense, there is truth in this opinion. If there be any pattern, purpose or direction in history, all counter-movements will, historically, be regarded as conspiracies against that nature or destiny. On the other hand, only those who fully believe in a transcendental predestination can avoid conspiracy, for they alone can rest in the confidence that it will be God's work.[4]

But it is his warning to "destiny" thinkers which is crucial. Without this, men face great temptation:

But to represent destiny in any sense does not mean to represent either perfect virtue or infallibility. The Bible points clearly to the wretched nature of the chosen people of the Old Covenant, and the heresies and sins of the elect people of the New Covenant. The various commanding empires of history, from Rome to the United States today, have not been preserved from grievous sins at their highest points. No party, religious group, or race, however confident of its cause and destiny, can afford the luxury of assuming that the righteousness of a cause a man affirms is identical with his own nature. The answer, on the other hand, is not mutual tolerance, for unity and brotherhood movements are either desertions of one's position for the religion of humanity, or else they are hypocrisy. The answer is not to be *one*, but to be *under law* rather than to claim to be *law incarnate*. It is the course of common sense to see one's real enemies as dangerous and evil, but it is also the course of wisdom to see oneself as a sinner, different only to the extent that God's grace is operative in us.[5]

---

4. R. J. Rushdoony, *The Nature of the American System* (Fairfax, Virginia: Thoburn Press, [1965] 1978), p. 144.

5. *Ibid.*, pp. 144–45.

In contrast to those who hide in darkness because their deeds are evil (John 3:19), let us follow the commission Jesus gave to His disciples concerning *open covenants openly arrived at*: "Ye are the light of the world. A city that is set on an hill cannot be hid. Neither do men light a candle, and put it under a bushel, but on a candlestick; and it giveth light unto all that are in the house. Let your light so shine before men, that they may see your good works, and glorify your Father which is in heaven" (Matthew 5:14–16).

What should our strategy be? At the very least, we ought to adopt this as our political minimum, our non-negotiable demand: "My hand out of your wallet; your hand out of my wallet; no handouts from the government; and handcuffs for the thieves."

Offensive Weapons

You can't beat something with nothing. The only thing that can defeat a bad idea is a good idea. We have the best ideas. We have the Bible, the U.S. Constitution, and an understanding of freedom. Freedom works. It produces abundance. Socialism produces poverty. It exists only because Western capitalists and governments have subsidized it with taxpayers' money. The Marxists have had to construct barbed wire defenses against people who would otherwise try to escape from socialist paradise.

What we need to understand is that the conflict is not merely a matter of logic. It is a matter of faith. The enemy within our gates are increasingly proponents of occultism. There is an alliance between secular humanism and outright occultism. This alliance goes back to the beginning of time. In the West, it goes back to the Renaissance, something admitted by professional historians only since about 1964. This is why Christians are uniquely equipped to fight this battle. They know that the weapons are spiritual. We need to put on the armor of God (Ephesians 6).

It must begin with knowledge. This is why I have written a full-length study of the forces arrayed against us: *Unholy Spirits: Occultism and New Age Humanism* (1986).[6] Until Christians understand the nature of the confrontation, they will continue to tilt at windmills.

The kind of information Christians need is not usually available in bookstores. Not in Christian bookstores, because Christian bookstores rarely have carried books like Quigley's *Tragedy and Hope*, Allen's *None Dare Call It Conspiracy*, and Billington's *Fire in the Minds of Men*. (Some now carry Pat Robertson's *New World Order*. Part 2 is such a good introduction that the book was widely criticized by the liberal press, unlike his other books, which have received little media attention.) Humanist bookstores seldom carry books like my *Unholy Spirits*. The books I list in my bibliography are usually out of print and are hard to locate, even in large university libraries. If it were not for copyright problems, I would put a lot of them on a CD-ROM.

Nevertheless, you need to read. He who refuses to read will be in a poor position to lead. If we think our opponents have done a terrible job, then we need to prepare ourselves to do a better job. They've done their homework. Are we doing ours?

It is time to sign up for a religious war that will last for the rest of your life. If we do our work faithfully, maybe we will start seeing some major victories before we get very far into the next millennium. I think we will. I smell victory. I think the enemy, for the first time in a century, has begun to smell defeat. They are trying to speed up their timetable because their dream of a one-world order is unravelling. Technology is now against them: decentralization. Newsletters are multiplying: alternative information sources. The World Wide Web is beyond anyone's control. The public schools are disintegrating. And millions of people are catching on. This is good news for God's people and bad news for His enemies.

---

6. Today published by the Institute for Christian Economics.

Appendix

MONITORING THE ELITE'S PUBLIC FACES

If this little book has made any impression on you whatsoever, it has at least raised your level of curiosity. Is the story in this book true or not? If you have asked yourself this question, let alone answered it for yourself, you should also have concluded: "I need more information."

Go right to the primary sources. Contact the several of these organizations and begin to examine what they say publicly about themselves. Then, if you become seriously interested, you should take time to monitor the public activities and published plans of one or more of them. Since they have gone to the expense of creating a public image, we should at least pay attention to this public side of their activities. All it takes is a letter to them (preferably typed, single spaced, return address in upper right-hand side) asking to receive a list of their various materials.

Order a copy of the *Annual Report* of the Council on Foreign Relations. Address your request to:

Council on Foreign Relations
The Harold Pratt House
58 East 68 Street
New York, NY 10021

You can also get on the mailing list of the Trilateral Commission. All it takes is a letter to them. They publish *Trialogue*, Triangle Papers, and other books and materials. Send your inquiry to

> Trilateral Commission
> 345 East 46th Street
> New York, NY 10017

On a much more personal level of recruiting is the Aspen Institute, located in Aspen, Colorado. This organization is aimed at business leaders, educators, and similar molders of opinion. They publish books and papers.

> The Aspen Institute for Humanistic Studies
> 1000 N. 3rd Street
> Aspen, CO 81611

Outside the United States, one of the most important organizations is the Royal Institute of International Affairs. Prof. Quigley believed that it was this organization which more or less served as the original model of the C.F.R. This organization is sometimes known as Chatham House, the building in which it is housed. There is a sister organization in each of the British Commonwealth nations.

> The Royal Institute of International Affairs
> Chatham House
> 10 St. James Square
> London, England SW1Y 4LE

BIBLIOGRAPHY

The bibliography on conspiracies is large, much larger than what I refer to here, but it is also obscure. The books come and go, but rarely do they stay in print for very long. The exposés are written by critics of the organizations. Few of them are formally trained historians or social scientists. The exceptions to this rule tend to be Marxists and new left historians. The conventional histories are written by men who probably know about the personal and economic connections that have made possible certain groups' exercise of power, but the authors are careful not to emphasize these connections. They may tell you that a group of men had great influence, but they do not explain why. Above all, they do not follow the money. Isaacson and Thomas's book, *The Wise Men*, is a representative example. Why were these six men so powerful in foreign policy circles (especially "Chip" Bohlen)? We are not told. The biographies of Eluhu Root, Henry L. Stimson, and John J. McCloy are sometimes large, yet they reveal remarkably little about the personal connections by which these three men wielded power. These three men were the unofficial chairmen of the unofficial American Establishment, each in succession, followed by David Rockefeller, McCloy's "protégé," according to McCloy's biographer. How did they gain their influence? Endless repetitions of the phrase "public service" conceal rather than explain.

When we consider the amount of ink and media time devoted to the Watergate break-in, an event which brought down a

President but whose perpetrators' actual motivation was never clearly explained, we should be curious. If all that media coverage and the millions of dollars of government investigative money did not reveal an acceptable answer as to why the break-in occurred, think of the really important political events of history. How can we make sense of them? How can we discovered what really happened and why it happened? For example, could the Watergate break-in really have been engineered by John Dean in order to learn whether the Democrats had learned of his new wife's possible connection to a prostitution ring, which is the thesis of Colodny and Gettlin's *Silent Coup* (St. Martin's, 1991)? If so, then there was less to Watergate than the investigators had imagined, and the fallout from it was remarkable when compared to this information's importance to Richard Nixon.

The Watergate investigation became a media extravaganza that seemed to elevate the reporter's calling to national status. Yet some of the details of the Watergate investigation raise questions that only hard-core conspiracy buffs ever ask. For instance, we all know that Nixon was brought down because of the White House audiotapes. But he refused to give up these tapes in one fell swoop. In fact, not until 1996 were scholars given access to these tapes. Only under specific demands by government prosecutors did Nixon turn over limited sections of those tapes. Gary Allen in 1976 summarized the findings of Susan Huck's February, 1975, article in *American Opinion*, the publication of the John Birch Society. Allen wrote in *The Kissinger File* (p. 179):

> Consider the fantastic detail involved in the requests. On August 14th, for example, Judge Sirica demanded the "entire segment of tape on the reel identified as 'White House telephone start 5/25/72 (2:00 P.M.) (skipping 8 lines) 6/23/72 (2:50 P.M.) (832) complete.' " I don't know what all the identifying numbers mean—but you have to agree that only somebody very familiar

with the tapes *would* know. These boys knew *precisely* what to look for! Here is another sample request:

January 8, 1973 from 4:05 to 5:34 P.M. (E.O.B.)
a)   at approximately 10 minutes and 15 seconds into the conversation, a segment lasting 6 minutes and 31 seconds:
b)   at approximately 67 minutes into the conversation, a segment lasting 11 minutes;
c)   at approximately 82 minutes and 15 seconds into the conversation, a segment lasting 5 minutes and 31 seconds.

Only Susan Huck asked the obvious question: How did the prosecutors know precisely when these incriminating discussions took place? There are only two possible answers: (1) someone with access to the tapes inside the White House was leaking the information; (2) there was a secret back-up set of the tapes in the hands of someone who was leaking the information. Leaked information would have been illegal for prosecutors to use in court, yet this was how they brought Nixon down.

To my knowledge, no reporter or professional historian has ever bothered to follow up on this remarkable oddity, or even mention it. Nobody ever asked: "What person was in charge of storing those tapes?" It took one of the least known and most diligent conspiracy historians (Ph.D. in geography) even to mention the problem. Strange? Not at all. Normal, in fact. Such is the nature of history and the writing of history whenever the events in question point to the operation of powerful people whose private interests are advanced by what appear to be honorable public activities that cost a lot of money.

Not every exposé is equally reliable in its assessment of the facts. Similarly, not every conventional history is equally innocuous in what it reveals. Even a poorly researched exposé can alert us to things to look up in conventional histories.

Exposés

Abraham, Larry. *Call It Conspiracy*. Seattle: Double A Press, 1985.

Abraham, Larry (with Franklin Sanders). *The Greening*. Atlanta, Georgia: Soundview, 1993.

Allen, Gary. *Jimmy Carter, Jimmy Carter*. Seal Beach, California: '76 Press, 1976.

Allen, Gary. *Kissinger: The Secret Side of the Secretary of State*. Seal Beach, California: '76 Press, 1976.

Allen, Gary. *Nixon's Palace Guard*. Boston: Western Islands, 1971.

Allen, Gary. *None Dare Call It Conspiracy*. Seal Beach, California: Concord, 1972.

Allen, Gary. *Richard Nixon: The Man Behind the Mask*. Boston: Western Islands, 1971.

Allen, Gary. *The Rockefeller File*. Seal Beach, California: '76 Press, 1976.

Allen, Gary. *Say "No" to the New World Order*. Seal Beach, California: Concord, 1987.

Bell, Don. *How the Barbarians Captured the Beloved Country*. Palm Beach, Florida: Don Bell Reports, 1966.

Finder, Joseph. *Red Carpet*. New York: Holt, Rinehart & Winston, 1983.

Higham, Charles. *Trading With the Enemy: An Exposé of the American Money Plot, 1933–1949*. New York: Delacorte, 1983.

Hoar, William. P. *Architects of Conspiracy: An Intriguing History*. Boston: Western Islands, 1984.

Griffin, G. Edward. *The Fearful Master: A Second Look at the United Nations*. Boston: Western Islands, 1964.

Groseclose, Elgin. *America's Money Machine: The Story of the Federal Reserve*. Westport, Connecticut: Arlington House, [1966] 1980.

Josephson, Emanuel M. *The "Federal" Reserve Conspiracy and Rockefeller: Their "Gold Corner"*. New York: Chedney, 1968.

Josephson, Emanuel M. *The Truth About Rockefeller: Public Enemy No. 1: Studies in Criminal Psychology*. New York: Chedney, 1964.

Kjos, Berit. *Brave New Schools*. Eugene, Oregon: Harvest House, 1995.

Levinson, Charles. *Vodka Cola*. London: Gordon & Cremonesi, 1978.

Liggio, Leonard and Martin, James J., eds. *Watershed of Empire: Essays on New Deal Foreign Policy*. Colorado Springs: Ralph Myles Press, 1976.

Lundberg, Ferdinand. *The Rich and the Super-Rich: A Study in the Power of Money Today*. New York: Lyle Stuart, 1968.

Lundberg, Ferdinand. *The Rockefeller Syndrome*. Secaucus, New Jersey: Lyle Stuart, 1975.

Martin, James J. *The Saga of Hog Island, And Other Essays in Inconvenient History*. Colorado Springs: Ralph Myles Press, 1977.

Martin, Rose. *Fabian Freeway: High Road to Socialism in the U.S.A.* Boston: Western Islands, 1966.

North, Gary. *Crossed Fingers: How the Liberals Captured the Presbyterian Church*. Tyler, Texas: Institute for Christian Economics, 1996.

Perloff, James. *The Shadows of Power: The Council on Foreign Relations and the American Decline*. Appleton, Wisconsin: Western Islands, 1988.

Reece Committee, *Tax-Exempt Foundations*. 83rd Congress, 2d Session, Report No. 2681, Dec. 16, 1954.

Robertson, Pat. *The New World Order*, Part 2. Dallas: Word, 1991.

Roosevelt, Archibald B. and Dobbs, Zygmund. *The Great Deceit: Social Pseudo-Sciences*. West Sayville, New York: Veritas Foundation, 1964.

Rothbard, Murray N. *The Case Against the Fed*. Auburn, Alabama: Mises Institute, 1994.

Rothbard, Murray N. *Wall Street, Banks, and American Foreign Policy*. Auburn, Alabama: Mises Institute, 1995.

Rushdoony, Rousas J. *The Biblical Philosophy of History*. Nutley, New Jersey: Presbyterian & Reformed, 1969.

Rushdoony, Rousas J. *The Nature of the American System*, Chapter VIII: "The Conspiracy View of History." Fairfax, Virginia: Thoburn Press, [1965] 1978.

Sargent, Porter. *Getting US into War*. Boston: Porter Sargent, 1941.

Scott, Otto. *The Other End of the Lifeboat*, Part 1. Chicago: Regnery, 1985.

Scott, Otto. *The Secret Six: John Brown and the Abolitionist Movement*. New York: Times Books, 1979. Reprinted by Uncommon Books, P. O. Box 69006, Seattle, Washington, 98168.

Sklar, Holly, ed. *Trilateralism: The Trilateral Commission and Elite Planning for World Management*. Boston: South End Press, 1980.

Skousen, W. Cleon. *The Naked Capitalist*. Salt Lake City: Privately Published, 1970.

Smoot, Dan. *The Invisible Government*. Dallas: Dan Smoot Report, 1962.

Stang, Alan. *The Actor: The True Story of John Foster Dulles, Secretary of State, 1953–1959*. Boston: Western Islands, 1968.

Sutton, Antony. *America's Secret Establishment: An Introduction to the Order of Skull & Bones*. Billings, Montana: Liberty House, 1986.

Sutton, Antony. *The Best Enemy Money Can Buy*. Billings, Montana: Liberty House, 1986.

Sutton, Antony. *Wall Street and the Bolshevik Revolution*. New Rochelle, New York: Arlington House, 1974.

Sutton, Antony. *Wall Street and FDR*. New Rochelle, New York: Arlington House, 1975.

Sutton, Antony. *Wall Street and the Rise of Hitler*. Seal Beach, California: '76 Press, 1976.

Sutton, Antony and Wood, Patrick. *Trilaterals Over Washington*. 2 vols. Scottsdale, Arizona: August Corp., 1978, 1981

Tarpley, Webster Griffin and Chaitkin, Anton. *George Bush: The Unauthorized Biography*. Washington, D.C.: Executive Intelligence Review, 1992.

van der Pijl, Kees. *The Making of an Atlantic Ruling Class*. London: Verso, 1984.

Webster, Nesta. *The French Revolution: A Study in Democracy*. 3rd edition; London: Constable, 1923.

Wormser, René. *Foundations: Their Power and Influence*. New York: Devin-Adair, 1958.

Conventional Histories

Abramson, Rudy. *Spanning the Century: The Life of W. Averell Harriman, 1891–1986*. New York: William Morrow, 1992.

Aldrich, Nelson W. *Old Money: The Mythology of America's Ruling Class*. New York: Knopf, 1988.

Attali, Jacques. *A Man of Influence: The Extraordinary Career of S. G. Warburg*. Bethesda, Maryland: Adler & Adler, 1987.

Barnet, Richard J. *The Alliance: America-Europe-Japan: Makers of the Postwar World*. New York: Simon & Schuster, 1983.

Billington, James. *Fire in the Minds of Men: Origins of the Revolutionary Faith*. New York: Basic Books, 1980.

Bird, Kai. *The Chairman: John J. McCloy: The Making of the American Establishment*. New York: Simon & Schuster, 1992.

Burch, Philip. H. *Elites in American History*. 3 vols. New York: Holmes & Meier, 1980.

Callahan, David. *Dangerous Capabilities: Paul Nitze and the Cold War*. New York: Edward Burlingame Book (HarperCollins*Publishers*), 1990.

Chandler, Lester V. *Benjamin Strong: Central Banker*. New York: Arno Press, [1958] 1979.

Chernow, Ron. *The House of Morgan: An American Banking Dynasty and the Rise of Modern Finance*. New York: Atlantic Monthly Press, 1990.

Collier, Peter and Horowitz, David. *The Rockefellers: An American Dynasty*. New York: Holt, Rinehart & Winston, 1976.

Current, Richard N. *Secretary Stimson: A Study in Statecraft*. New Brunswick, New Jersey: Rutgers University Press, 1954.

Deacon, Richard. *The Cambridge Apostles: A history of Cambridge University's élite intellectual secret society*. London: Robert Royce, 1985.

Domhoff, G. William. *Who Rules America Now?: A View for the '80s*. Englewood Cliffs, New Jersey: Prentice-Hall, 1983.

Duchene, Francois. *Jean Monnet: The First Statesman of Interdependence*. New York: Norton, 1994.

Fisher, Don. *Fundamental Development of the Social Sciences: Rocke-feller Philanthropy and the United States Social Science Research Council*. Ann Arbor: University of Michigan Press, 1993.

Fosdick, Raymond B. *John D. Rockefeller, Jr., A Portrait*. New York: Harper & Bros., 1956.

Funigello, Philip J. *American-Soviet Trade in the Cold War*. Chapel Hill: University of North Carolina Press, 1988.

Harr, John Ensor and Johnson, Peter J. *The Rockefeller Century*. New York: Scribner's, 1988.

Heald, Tim. *Old Boy Networks: Who We Know and How We Use Them*. New York: Ticknor & Fields, 1984.

Hiebert, Ray Eldon. *Courtier to the Crowd: The Story of Ivy Lee and the Development of Public Relations*. Ames, Iowa: Iowa State University Press, 1966.

Hodgson, Godfrey. *The Colonel: The Life and Wars of Henry Stimson, 1867–1950*. New York: Knopf, 1990.

Isaacson, Walter and Thomas, Evan. *The Wise Men: Six Friends and the World They Made: Acheson, Bohlen, Harriman, Kennan, Lovett, McCloy*. New York: Simon & Schuster, 1986.

Jessup, Philip C. *Elihu Root*. 2 vols. Archon Books, [1938] 1964.

Johnson, George. *Architects of Fear: Conspiracy Theories and Para-noia in American Politics*. Los Angeles: Tarcher, 1983.

Kolko, Gabriel. *The Triumph of Conservatism: A Reinterpretation of American History, 1900–1916*. New York: Free Press of Glencoe, 1963.

Lamont, Thomas W. *Henry P. Davison: The Record of a Useful Life*. New York: Harper & Bros., 1933.

Lisagor, Nancy and Lipsius, Frank. *A Law Unto Itself: The Untold Story of the Law Firm of Sullivan & Cromwell*. New York: William Morrow, 1988.

Marlowe, John. *Milner: Apostle of Empire*. London: Hamish Hamilton, 1976.

McCartney, Laton. *Friends in High Places: The Bechtel Story: The Most Secret Corporation and How It Engineered the World*. New York: Simon & Schuster, 1988.

Miller, Arthur S. *The Secret Constitution and the Need for Constitutional Change*. Westport, Connecticut: Greenwood, 1987.

Pussey, Merlo J. *Eugene Meyer*. New York: Knopf, 1974.

Quigley, Carroll. *The Anglo-American Establishment*. New York: Books in Focus, 1981. Reprinted by GSC & Associates, P. O. Box 6448-Eastview Station, San Pedro, California 90734.

Quigley, Carroll. *Tragedy and Hope: A History of the World in Our Time*, pp. 936–56. New York: Macmillan, 1966. Reprinted by GSC & Associates, P. O. Box 6448-Eastview Station, San Pedro, California 90734.

Steel, Ronald. *Walter Lippmann and the American Century*. New York: Vintage, 1981.

Stephenson, Nathaniel Wright. *Nelson W. Aldrich: A Leader in American Politics*. New York: Kennikat, [1930] 1971.

Wells, H. G. *The Open Conspiracy: Blue Prints for a World Revolution*. Garden City, New York: Doubleday, Doran, 1928.

Primary Sources

The Freemen Digest, Salt Lake City, published a remarkable series of magazine-length reports in 1978 and 1979. The researcher gained the cooperation of many Insider organizations, which shared their documents with him and agreed to their publication without editorial comment. I am informed by Cleon Skousen, the publisher, that the Council on Foreign Relations was so pleased with its report that it ordered thousands of extra copies to be placed in libraries around the world. Unfortunately, the project ended prior to the researcher's release of the materials on that most important of all international organizations, the Bank for International Settlements, which had supplied him with reams of material. The published reports included:

Aspen Institute for Humanistic Studies (1979)
Atlantic Institute for International Affairs (1979)
Bilderberg Meetings (1978)
Council on Foreign Relations (1979)
European Economic Community (1979)
Fabian Society (1979)
Institutes for International Affairs (1979)
Trilateral Commission (1979)
Trilateralism (1979)

SCRIPTURE INDEX

INDEX

ABOUT THE AUTHOR

Gary North received his Ph.D. in history from the University of California, Riverside, in 1972. He specialized in colonial U.S. history. He wrote his doctoral dissertation on Puritan New England's economic history and the history of economic thought. A simplified version of this dissertation has been published as *Puritan Economic Experiments* (Institute for Christian Economics, 1988).

He is the author of approximately 43 books in the fields of economics, history, and theology. His first book, *Marx's Religion of Revolution*, appeared in 1968. His *Introduction to Christian Economics* appeared in 1973, the year he began writing a multi-volume economic commentary on the Bible, which now covers Genesis, Exodus (three volumes), Leviticus, and Numbers. He was the general editor of the Biblical Blueprints Series (1986-87), a 10-volume set, for which he wrote four of the books. He is the author of *Crossed Fingers: How the Liberals Captured the Presbyterian Church* (1996), which he began in 1962.

Beginning in 1965, his articles and reviews have appeared in over three dozen newspapers and periodicals, including the *Wall Street Journal*, *Modern Age*, *Journal of Political Economy*, *National Review*, and *The Freeman*.

He edited the first fifteen issues of *The Journal of Christian Reconstruction*, 1974-81. He edited a *festschrift* for Cornelius Van Til, *Foundations of Christian Scholarship* (1976). He edited two issues of *Christianity and Civilization* in 1983: *The Theology of Christian Resistance* and *Tactics of Christian Resistance*. He edited *Theonomy: An Informed Response* (1991).

He is the editor of the monthly financial newsletter, *Remnant Review*. He writes two bi-monthly Christian newsletters, *Biblical Economics Today* and *Christian Reconstruction*, published by the Institute for Christian Economics.

He lives in Tyler, Texas, with his wife and four children.

Free E-Mail Subscriptions

For a free e-mail subscription to Gary North's monthly news-letters, *Biblical Economics Today* and *Christian Reconstruction*, each published every other month, e-mail to:

list-request@metanet.net

Write **subscribe ice-list** in the text box.

The Great Tribulation
by David Chilton

Some questions that many of today's Christians want the answers to: "Are we living in the Last Days?" "Are the signs of our times the Signs of the End?" "Is the Great Tribulation just around the corner?"

For centuries, Christians have sought to interpret the Bible's scriptural meaning of events referred to in Revelation as "the great tribulation" – often erroneously assigning modern ideology to scriptural passages. *The Great Tribulation* is perhaps the most comprehensive and easily understood writing available on this cataclysmic event "which so many Christians are awaiting." As Chilton proves however, it will be a long wait, since this event occurred in A.D. 70. It fell upon Jerusalem, not the church. It's over.

This book is an excellent tool for modern man in learning how Scripture interprets Scripture. It is also a good book to give to your fundamentalist friends. It's just what they think they're looking for: more hot news on the crisis that lies ahead! *Wait until they find out they've been conned for 20 years.* They have been, after all.

195 pp., indexed, paperback, $5.95
Dominion Press, P.O. Box 7999, Tyler, Texas 75711

Order all five books advertised here ($106. value) for $80.00 and pay no shipping costs. Send a check to: Dominion Press, P.O. Box 7999, Tyler, TX 75711

Paradise Restored:
A Biblical Theology of Dominion
by David Chilton

In recent years many Christians have begun to realize a long forgotten truth: God wants us to have dominion over the earth, just as He originally commanded Adam and Eve. By His atonement, Jesus Christ has restored us to Adam's lost position, guaranteeing that God's original plan will be fulfilled. God will be glorified throughout the world: *"The earth shall be full of the knowledge of the LORD, as the waters cover the sea."* Isaiah 11:9.

In order to demonstrate this truth from Scripture, David Chilton begins at the beginning, in the Garden of Eden. He shows how God established basic patterns in the first few chapters of Genesis – patterns which form the structure of later Biblical revelation. In the course of this book on eschatology, the reader is treated to an exciting, refreshingly *Biblical* way of reading the Bible.

Building on a solid foundation of New Testament eschatology, the author deals at length with the message of the Book of Revelation – often with surprising results. Throughout the volume, the reader is confronted with the fact that our view of the *future* is inescapably bound up with our view of Jesus Christ. According to the author, the fact that Jesus is *now* King of kings and Lord of lords means that His Gospel must be victorious: the Holy Spirit will bring the water of life to the ends of the earth. The Christian message is one of Hope.

342 pp., indexed, bibliography, paperback, $17.95
Dominion Press, P.O. Box 7999, Tyler, Texas 75711

Order all five books advertised here ($106. value) for $80.00 and pay no shipping costs. Send a check to: Dominion Press, P.O. Box 7999, Tyler, TX 75711

Days of Vengeance
An Exposition of the Book of Revelation
by David Chilton

This is quite possibly the most comprehensive verse by verse treatment of the Book of Revelation ever written. David Chilton has tackled what Calvin and Luther never even attempted. Following in the train of thought of his *Paradise Restored,* Chilton sees the Church triumphant to the end with Satan defeated at the return of Christ. The Apostle John presents a vision of victorious Christians who overcome all opposition through the work of Jesus Christ. Chilton asserts that for too long the Church has labored under the delusion that failure is her only role in the world. An inviting, yet non-threatening commentary for the layman as well as the scholar.

721 pp., indexed, hardback, $24.95
Dominion Press, P.O. Box 7999, Tyler, Texas 75711

Political Polytheism:
The Myth of Pluralism
by Gary North

No political order can be religiously neutral, and the modern political order in the United States and other Western nations, called "pluralism," is in reality polytheism. As in the ancient world, polytheists are offended at those who claim that there is only one God, and this is why orthodox Christianity is increasingly under assault in the United States and throughout the Western world. In this book, Gary North brings his many years of theological and historical research to bear on the question of how this polytheistic state of affairs came about, and what must be done about it. In a powerful argument, sure to be controversial, North points a finger at the framers of the Constitution of the United States, who self-consciously broke with 1000 + years of Western heritage by not referring to the Trinity and to Christ as King. This was the hole in the dike, North contends, through which modern secularism has poured. No one concerned about the state of the American nation can afford to ignore this book.

795 pp., indexed, hardback, $22.50
Institute for Christian Economics, P.O. Box 8000, Tyler, TX 75711

Order all five books advertised here ($106. value) for $80.00 and pay no shipping costs. Send a check to: Dominion Press, P.O. Box 7999, Tyler, TX 75711

Crossed Fingers
How the Liberals Captured the Presbyterian Church
by Gary North

This book is the first to detail the step-by-step program of infiltration used by modernists to take over the Northern Presbyterian Church. Other books have chronicled the results of this program, but none has shown how it was done. The infiltration process began as early as 1870, and it culminated in the expulsion of the conservatives in 1936. This book shows that the modernists held a systematic theology that was a perverse mirror image of the Presbyterianism of the Westminster Confession. It presents the compromised midway theology of the majority wing of the Church: New School Presbyterians and fundamentalists (after 1910). It also shows why the conservatives were unwilling to defend the Westminster Confession through court actions against heretics except in the 1890's, and even then, they refused to deal with many of the fundamental theological issues. The conservatives, from Charles Hodge to J. Gresham Machen, were themselves unwilling to accept all of the Confession, especially in the key area of creationism. Because they crossed their fingers when they swore allegiance to the Confession, the modernists also crossed theirs, and all but six of them got away with it. The conservatives were outfoxed time after time.Then, after 1907, the conservatives consented to a series of tactical moves that passed institutional power to the modernists and their pietistic allies. They did not understand what they had done until two decades after they had done it. By then, it was too late. This book also lists a series of red-alert signals that point to a replay of the liberals' strategy.

1096 pp., indexed, hardback, $34.95
Institute for Christian Economics, P.O. Box 8000, Tyler, Texas 75711